D0992902

## SEMINAR STUDIES IN HISTORY

Editor: Patrick Richardson

# LEFT AND RIGHT IN TWENTIETH-CENTURY EUROPE

# SEMINAR STUDIES IN HISTORY

Editor: Patrick Richardson

A full list of titles in this
series will be found on the
back cover of this book

SEMINAR STUDIES IN HISTORY

# LEFT AND RIGHT IN TWENTIETH-CENTURY EUROPE

David Smith

**LONGMAN**

**LONGMAN GROUP LIMITED**
London

ASSOCIATED COMPANIES, BRANCHES AND
REPRESENTATIVES THROUGHOUT THE WORLD

© Longman Group Ltd 1970

First published 1970
New impression 1973

ISBN 0582 31408 9

PRINTED IN GREAT BRITAIN BY
LOWE AND BRYDONE (PRINTERS) LTD.,
THETFORD, NORFOLK

# Contents

# Introduction to the Series

The seminar method of teaching is being used increasingly in VI forms and at universities. It is a way of learning in smaller groups through discussion, designed both to get away from and to supplement the basic lecture techniques. To be successful, the members of a seminar must be informed, or else—in the unkind phrase of a cynic, it can be a 'pooling of ignorance'. The chapter in the textbook of English or European history by its nature cannot provide material in this depth, but at the same time the full academic work may be too long and perhaps too advanced for students at this level.

For this reason we have invited practising teachers in universities, schools and colleges of further education to contribute short studies on specialised aspects of British and European history with these special needs and pupils of this age in mind. For this series the authors have been asked to provide, in addition to their basic analysis, a full selection of documentary material of all kinds and an up-to-date and comprehensive bibliography. Both these sections are referred to in the text, but it is hoped that they will prove to be valuable teaching and learning aids in themselves.

*Note on the System of References:*

A bold number in round brackets (**5**) in the text refers the reader to the corresponding entry in the Bibliography section at the end of the book.

A bold number in square brackets, preceded by 'doc.' [**docs 6, 8**] refers the reader to the corresponding items in the section of Documents, which follows the main text.

PATRICK RICHARDSON
General Editor

# Acknowledgements

We are grateful to the following for permission to reproduce copyright material:

George Allen & Unwin Ltd for extracts from *Reflections on Violence* by George Sorel, translated by T. E. Hulme; Cambridge University Press for extracts from *The Social and Political Doctrines of Contemporary Europe* by M. Oakeshott; The Communist Party of Great Britain for extracts from *The Theory and Practice of Leninism* by J. V. Stalin; author's agents, Miss Sonia Brownell, Secker and Warburg Ltd and Harcourt, Brace Jovanovich for extracts from *Homage to Catalonia* by George Orwell, copyright 1952 by Sonia Brownell Orwell; Hodder and Stoughton Ltd and Raymond Savage Ltd for extracts from *Failure of a Mission* by Sir Nevile Henderson; Hutchinson & Co. Ltd for extracts from *Mein Kampf* by Adolf Hitler, translated by J. Murphy; Lawrence and Wishart Ltd and International Publishers Inc. for extracts from *What is to be Done* and *State and Revolution* by Lenin; Librairie Artheme Fayard for extracts from *Mes Idées Politiques* by Charles Maurras.

# Part One

# BACKGROUND
# AND THEORY

# 1 Background

In the early days of February 1934 the Marxist Social Democrats of Vienna declared a general strike. In retaliation the Catholic conservative government of Dr Engelbert Dollfuss, actively supported by the paramilitary forces of the Fascist *Heimwehr*, launched a military bombardment of the Karl Marx House and the Goethe House, two blocks of workers' dwellings erected by the Socialist city government. The tenements were destroyed and along with them the Viennese Socialist movement. Almost a thousand men, women and children were killed. The leader of the *Heimwehr*, Prince Ernst von Starhemberg, shortly afterwards became Vice-Chancellor and a new constitution brought both trade unions and parliamentary government in Austria to an end.

This incident, occurring four years before the German annexation of Austria, is not the best known event of this period in European history but it is tragically characteristic. In the short period after the war 'to end war' and 'make the world safe for democracy' Europe was torn apart by such civil conflicts and parliamentary democracy went into eclipse. Where the left or, more often, the right triumphed, the traditions of freedom, tolerance and the rule of law were swept aside by totalitarian régimes whose iron grip extended across every organ of government and every aspect of social life, winning acquiescence or stifling opposition by a combination of propaganda and police terror.

The purpose of this essay is not to record these events in detail, something which has already been done in innumerable textbooks and which can be pursued further with the aid of the bibliography. Its aim is rather to raise questions about their significance. What created these bitter animosities? What social forces lay behind them? What factors imparted such passion and such inhumanity to politics? What persuaded Europe to desert the traditions of parliamentary democracy and what did it gain in return?

Such questions involve the study of political ideology and also of political sociology. They invite a comparison of what the politicians practised with what they preached. The enquiry should begin however with some preliminary definitions of terms. What was the left? What was the right? What was the apparently irreconcilable difference between them?

The terms are familiar and even overworked in historical and political discussion. They entered European politics at the time of the French Revolution. In the National Assembly of 1789 a division of views soon made itself apparent over the question of the royal veto. One section of the members took the radical view that the will of the elected representatives of the people should prevail on questions of reform. Another, composed of the nobility and higher clergy, upheld royal power. The first of these groups sat or stood to the left of the speaker's chair, the second to the right. In the centre, before the speaker, gathered moderate and uncommitted men. The extremists agreed in condemning their moderation as a weakness springing from lack of principle or corrupt self-seeking.

This historical spectrum has become the classical stereotype of European political opinions. The left is radical, democratic and reforming. The right is resistant to change in these directions, even reactionary. The centre, in fortunate times, holds the balance. In times of crisis power falls to one or other of the extremes, usually not without a conflict.

Some time before the twentieth century began, however, the political and social consequences of European industrialisation had added a new dimension to the left. Marxist Socialists extended their radical demands beyond a popular franchise to a social revolution— the abolition of private property and the nationalisation or communalisation of 'the means of production, distribution and exchange'. These demands were made in tones of varying moderation and extremism. Some Socialists are less revolutionary than others not only in their methods but also in what they will accept as terms of settlement. In the twentieth century, however, Marxism has been the touch-stone of the left.

'The origin of the Right', says Ernst Nolte, 'lies always in the challenge of the Left' (47). Anti-Communism is the badge of the twentieth-century right. It was the motive force behind the attack on the Karl Marx House, behind the support which Mussolini and Hitler won, and behind the alliance of landowners, monarchists, prelates and army officers which Franco led to power in Spain. Centrally important as it is, this negative characteristic is not a complete description of the European right. Long before Communism clothed its spectral nineteenth-century form in twentieth-century flesh and blood the strident nationalism, the anti-semitism and the hostility towards liberal politics and liberal values which marked Fascism and Nazism had already appeared in Europe. Half a century before Vienna became the battleground of left and right it had been Hitler's school of political education in which, at least according to *Mein Kampf*, he formed his philosophy. In some respects, moreover, twentieth-century Fascism added a new dimension to the right. At least in theory many of its leaders were anti-capitalist as well as anti-Communist, as radical as the Marxists in their condemnation of social injustice and equally visionary in their promises of a new order.

This dynamic aspect of popular Fascism has led some historians to classify it as a phenomenon of the left, or rather to discard the old labels altogether. In practice, the radicalism of Fascism added up to much less than it preached. This may have been through force of circumstances or the necessary compromises of power, or because of a defect of intention. These are questions to which this essay will return. It is also possible that anti-Communism itself was a front, a bogey which Fascists were quick to brandish once they realised the extent and popularity of its appeal, just as Communists raise the cry of 'Fascist' when they wish for tactical purposes to form a popular front. Political ideology is treacherous ground for the student. In this essay, the right will be defined as the opposition to the Marxist left, the radical and extremist apposition which, along with its left opponents, was ready to abandon reason, toleration and even human decency in its political behaviour.

Politicians and their supporters do not resort to such means unless driven by powerful emotions of fear, hatred and hysteria. In seeking to understand the inspiration of the European left and right, it is the intensity of these feelings which must be considered and explained. The explanation lies in the nature of political ideology. 'The lack of a great idea which would reshape things anew', wrote Hitler, 'has always meant a limitation in fighting-power. The conviction of the right to employ even the most brutal weapons is always associated with an ardent faith for a new and revolutionary transformation of the world. A movement which does not fight for such high aims and ideals will never have recourse to extreme means' (**18**). The convictions and aims of the left and the right will be discussed respectively in chapters 2 and 3.

# 2 The Left in Theory

A dictionary defines ideology as 'a body of doctrine, myth and symbol with reference to some political and cultural plan along with the devices for putting it into operation'. Marxism is the doctrine of the twentieth-century left. Its myths and symbols are those of the class struggle, the proletarian revolution and the classless society. The dictionary notes an alternative definition of ideology however—'theorising of a visionary or impractical nature'—and this was the state of Marxism when the twentieth century began. Its call to the workers of the world to unite and revolt was half a century old, but they had not necessarily revolted and they were not united. Instead the Second Socialist International (1889–1914) was riven by arguments and factions, divisions which arose principally from the frustrations of political impotence. The Marxist writings had become sacred texts, the subject of scholastic wrangling and disputation, but seldom carried into consistent political action.

'Is social democracy today anything beyond a party that strives after the socialist transformation of society by the means of democratic and economic reform?' asked the German Socialist, Edouard Bernstein [**doc. 2**]. By 1914 the German Social Democratic party was the largest single party in the Reichstag. Its parliamentary and trade union strength and its parliamentary methods had obtained from Conservative governments a series of social and industrial reforms which began with Bismarck and made Germany the most comprehensive and advanced welfare state in Europe. It had not affected the structure of German capitalism, which similarly led Europe in its efficiency and productivity. Bernstein was asking socialists to face the realities of an advanced industrial society and, having done so, to abandon the essentially primitive ideas of a Socialist doctrine developed at a much earlier phase in that society's history. His 'revisionist' doctrine has been that of the moderate left in the advanced countries of western Europe such as Germany and Britain, and at every stage it has been supported by the majority of the politically conscious working class. It is clearly the product of a situation, however, and where less sophisticated social and political conditions exist it may be expected to be less popular. It also marks a conscious departure from the revolutionary myth, which Bernstein regarded as a notion having no relevance to real politics. For this reason his argument proved too frank for even his German fellow-Socialists to accept, and he was expelled.

Elsewhere in western Europe, industrialisation was still in its primitive and early phase and socialist politics were more authentically revolutionary. In Spain and in Italy the conditions of labour were hard and crude, the rewards were small and governments were unresponsive. In these countries, as in Russia, the proletariat were still at only a short remove from the peasant masses of the population and the discipline of the factory and the mine was resented most keenly. Socialism there was anarchist in its expression (**42**).

Anarchism is only partly Marxist in its inspiration. Indeed Marx was the inheritor of the anarchist tradition. The classless society in which both capitalism and the oppressive state have ceased to exist and in which men govern themselves in small communities is the anarchist myth. Marx introduced the concept of the dictatorship of the proletariat—an interim, post-revolutionary phase in which the working class will 'use its political supremacy to invert, by degrees, all capital from the bourgeoisie, to centralise all instruments of production in the hands of the state, i.e. of the proletariat organised as the ruling class; and to increase the total of productive forces as rapidly as possible' (**8**). This is the stage which Russian Communism has reached and from which it shows no historical or present signs of developing further. The Anarchist would not be surprised, for he condemned the method as defective from the start. Anarchism, which in industrial society has usually called itself syndicalism, favours direct action: the occupation by the workers of their factories and an immediate transfer of ownership to syndicates of producers. To call in the machinery of the state for this purpose, even momentarily, is to perpetuate bureaucratic oppression.

Extreme and visionary in its theories, violent in its methods, Anarcho-Syndicalism is emotionally a revolt against the industrialising and urbanising processes which historically have created modern European society. It wants to liberate man from his social and political environment. Since it rejects the course of history, it is reactionary in its inspiration as much as it is revolutionary. For this

B

reason its theories have provided inspiration for Fascism as well as for Socialism, for the right as well as for the left.

The leading theorist of early twentieth-century Anarcho-syndicalism was a retired French civil engineer, Georges Sorel. American and Italian socialists revered his work, as well as some French trade unionists, but Mussolini and the French Fascists also acknowledged a debt to him. Sorel despaired of European Socialism, which in France seemed to be taking the revisionist path even more enthusiastically than in Germany. French Socialists joined coalition cabinets as ministers. He also despaired of capitalism which, by its policies of wage concessions and social reform, seemed to have lost its teeth. He regarded the turbulent industrial relations of the United States of America with a perverse admiration. There employers shot down workers with the approval of the state and workers replied in kind.

> There are found the indomitable energy, the audacity based on a just appreciation of its strength, the cold calculation of interests, which are the qualities of great generals and great capitalists. . . . In a society so enfevered by the passion for the success which can be obtained in competition, all the actors walk straight before them like veritable automata, without taking notice of any of the great ideas of the sociologists; they are subject to very simple forces, and not one of them dreams of escaping from the circumstances of his condition (**14**) [**doc. 3**].

Sorel aimed to restore these primitive conditions of the class struggle to Europe. He wanted to detach Socialism from its gradualist and essentially bourgeois methods, and even from planning for a political revolution. He wished to substitute action for words and violence for moderation. Sorel was the first to realise the importance of ideology in creating the revolutionary state of mind. 'Lofty moral convictions', he wrote, 'never depend on reasoning or on any education of the individual will, but on a state of war in which men voluntarily participate and which finds expression in well-defined myths.' 'Myths', he commented, 'are not descriptions of things but expressions of a determination to act' (**14**).

This is the authentic language of twentieth-century ideological politics. Sorel urged men to act rather than to reflect and gave revolutionary violence the romantic aura of an heroic and religious crusade. He insisted that a preoccupation with the plans of a new society would destroy the purity of the revolution. The new forms would evolve from the action of revolution itself. In prophetic words, he warned against the concept of the dictatorship of the proletariat and the establishment of a revolutionary leadership élite:

> The men who had managed to organise the proletariat in the form of an army, ever ready to obey their orders, would be generals who would set up a state of siege in vanquished society: we should therefore have, on the day following the revolution, a dictatorship exercised by those politicians who, in the society of today, already form a compact group (**14**).

Anarchism, just because of its doctrinal purity, has remained on the fringes of twentieth-century politics. Communism organised for revolution and for power and achieved both. In this process Lenin was the key figure. Tsarist Russia was a country where the social conditions of incipient industrialisation were harsh, where most trade unions were illegal, and where parliamentary institutions did not exist until 1905 and remained weak thereafter. There were Socialist gradualists in Russia, 'legal' Marxists who argued that the proletarian revolution could not transpire until bourgeois parliamentarism had run its course and that the best policy, therefore, was one of cooperation with the bourgeois liberals of the Duma and, later, of the Provisional Government. Lenin rejected their theory: 'To decide every few years which member of the ruling class is to repress and oppress the people through Parliament, that is the real essence of middle-class parliamentarism, not only in parliamentary and constitutional Monarchies but also in the most democratic Republics' (**10**).

Lenin rejected a policy of trade union 'opportunism'. He also despised the Anarchists, both for their lack of practical sense and for their violent 'propaganda of the deed' which served only to increase the determination of established society not to yield. Lenin was the first to recognise the phenomenon of the right backlash. He was a revolutionary, but for him revolution was a long-term and practical business. The need was to organise. The title of one of the first and most famous of his pamphlets was *What is to be done?* (**9**).

What needed to be done, he argued, was to create 'an *organisation of revolutionaries* capable of maintaining the energy, the stability and continuity of the class struggle'. The function of such an organisation

9

was to arouse and concentrate the revolutionary consciousness of the masses,

> to be able to react to every manifestation of tyranny and oppression, no matter where it takes place, no matter what stratum or class of the people it affects; he must be able to group all these manifestations into a single picture of police violence and capitalist exploitation; he must be able to take advantage of every petty event in order to explain his socialistic convictions and his Social-Democratic demands to *all*, in order to explain to *all* and everyone the world-historic significance of the struggle for the emancipation of the proletariat (**9**) [**doc. 4a**].

The ultimate aim was revolution and the seizure of state power by the revolutionaries. Beyond that lay the establishment of a Communist society. The whole process was extended however, perhaps over a period of many years. The Communist played a waiting game, exercising restraint when it was necessary, operating in secrecy and underground when the times were unpropitious, and striking only when his political judgment indicated that the iron was hot.

Such tactics made considerable demands on the revolutionary will. They called for dedication, patience, secrecy and discipline. In a famous phrase Lenin described his organisation as 'a party of a new type' distinguished by the smallness of its membership and their obedience to the party line of tactics. Unreflecting action and prolonged argument were as foreign to its nature as they were unwelcome to Lenin's irascible and dominating personality. He was the first of the ideologists of the twentieth century to insist on the unquestioned authority of the leader over his followers. The implications of such a theory of socialist strategy were already clear to Sorel and they were voiced with equal foresight by the German Socialist leader, Rosa Luxemburg:

> Nothing will more surely enslave a young labour movement to an intellectual élite hungry for power than this bureaucratic straitjacket, which will immobilise the movement and turn it into an automaton manipulated by a Central Committee. . . . What is today only a phantom haunting Lenin's imagination may become reality tomorrow (**16**) [**doc. 10a**].

Lenin achieved power however. Rosa Luxemburg tried in vain by democratic methods to dissuade the German Communists not to launch their ill-fated revolution of 1919. Soon afterwards she was assassinated by the ex-officers of the emergent German right.

With Lenin's formulation of revolutionary tactics and the party of a new type, we have completed a review of the varieties of inspiration of the early twentieth-century left. With Lenin, too, the ideology of the left has emerged both from the moderation of parliamentarism and trade unionism and from the realm of theorising of a visionary or impractical nature. The left has become revolutionary and it has become real. It was soon to achieve power in Russia. This was the starting-point of the reaction from the right.

# 3 The Right in Theory

The right, in the terms in which this book deals, is principally defined by what it was against rather than by any more positive characteristics. As such, it may seem hardly an ideology at all but rather the reflex action of established social groups and the petty bourgeoisie against the threat of social revolution. The Communists defined Fascism in these terms: on various occasions it was called 'the praetorian guard of monopoly capitalism' and 'the terrorist dictatorship of the petty bourgeoisie'.

The Communists both overrated and underrated Fascism by these descriptions: overrated it because monopoly capitalism was cautious and grudging in its support on more than one occasion, and underrated it because Fascism exerted an appeal which extended across class barriers and even deprived Communism itself of some of the working-class support to which ideologically it regarded itself as entitled. One reason why the Vienna general strike of 1934 failed was that a substantial number of railway workers were members of the *Heimwehr*. Fascism and Nazism were more than one-class movements and there was more than anti-Communism to their ideology, although it was always their strongest card. An extended list of their ideological attributes nevertheless remains fuller of negative than of positive sentiments. Anti-parliamentarism, anti-semitism, anti-intellectualism, even anti-capitalism reflect the reactionary, vengeful and essentially petty nature of much right-wing political thought in the twentieth century. The sentiment of patriotism itself, which sounded passionately through the propaganda of the right, can be a negative and restricting emotion when it represents no more than arrogant chauvinism or ignorant and irrational prejudice against peoples of different language, race or colour.

Socialist ideology, as we have seen, developed different emphases according to the local circumstances of economic and political life. The glorification of the nation similarly prevented the ideology of the right from being alike in any two countries. A Fascist International was impossible, though ironically enough the leaders of the right made more effective alliances in practice than anything the left could manage. The spirit of nationalism is an outstanding common factor among the right-wing movements.

The senior ideologue of the early twentieth-century right was the Frenchman, Charles Maurras. This was not so much because of his influence, though in French politics it was and has remained pervasive, as because of the fact that his career as a political publicist, founder of the right-wing newspaper *Action Française*, began in the nineteenth century and extended through the second world war, when ironically the arch-patriot collaborated with the German invaders. This conclusion was ironic because Maurras's political thinking began with a patriotic indignation at the defeat of France in the Franco-Prussian war and her apparently continuing military weakness in the face of the new German empire. Why was France weak? In the manner which is the characteristic of ideological politicians, Maurras looked for a dramatic and simple answer. He looked for villains and found them among the bourgeois politicians of the Third Republic: 'France is destroyed because the government are not statesmen but men of party. If they are honest, they think only of the good of the party; if they are dishonest, they seek only to fill their pockets. Honest or dishonest, they are the enemies of France. France is not a party' [**doc. 5**].

The structure of French politics lent itself to this charge. A system of proportional representation results inevitably in a multiplicity of political parties and the governments which result are usually unstable coalitions. This affects the behaviour of politicians. If they support the government, they must be tempted to exploit their positions by demands for office or favours, threatening to withdraw their support if they are not satisfied. In opposition, they tend to be irresponsible, combining to bring down governments for petty reasons because they know they are unlikely to be called upon to form a government themselves, but can hope to bargain with whoever does. Such factors have introduced an almost permanent state of surface instability to French republican politics which derives, it is clear, as much from the system as from the men or the movements in political life. For Maurras, however, such a relatively impersonal explanation was insufficient. He focused on the personal inadequacies of politicians and connected these with the larger decline of France, though this in its turn seems to the historian a question of

13

the rate of economic development rather than of defective political leadership.

The weakness, according to Maurras, was disunity: the remedy was national unity. The villains were party politicians: the hero must be a man above party. Maurras reveals the nineteenth-century origins of his political thought when he looks back into history for such a man rather than to the charismatic dictators of the twentieth-century right. He called for the restoration of the French monarchy:

> Corruptible as a man in so many ways, the King has as king an immediate and obvious advantage in remaining uncorrupt: his rule of sensibility is to show himself insensible to everything which concerns only the individual, his interest is to be naturally detached from the interests which clamour about him. His interest is to make himself independent [**doc. 5**].

Apart from such theoretical arguments, the monarchy exercised another attraction. It symbolised the past greatness of royal, Catholic France. The almost permanent decline of France, or so it seemed to Maurras, had begun when France deserted her history and surrendered to the rule of 'Anti-France'—an unholy, conspiratorial quaternity of protestants, freemasons, Jews and foreign-born French citizens. The conspiracy theory of history is another strong characteristic of right-wing ideology which burst into an excited illusion of reality over the Dreyfus affair. So is the idea that nationality is more than a matter of passports. *La terre et les morts*, Maurras's definition of national identity, is exactly comparable with Nazism's *blut und boden*.

In other ways Maurras's ideology differs from that of twentieth-century Fascism. It was essentially nostalgic rather than modern, and aristocratic rather than popular. Its appeal was restricted, and the popular French Fascists such as Valois and Doriot abandoned its old-fashioned exclusiveness. *Action française* in turn despised them as demagogues. Ironically also, both the Catholic Church and the pretender to the throne of France disowned *Action française*, and it was never a positive political force which seemed likely to seize power. So long as France has experienced the instabilities and recurrent crises of its particular form of parliamentary government, however, the theory of the incorruptible leader has exercised powerful appeal, particularly when the threat of left revolution has been added to the situation.

The connection of the Catholic Church with right-wing politics has been and remains an obscure and controversial topic. The Church condemned Communism for its atheistic materialism, and as a secular body with considerable material wealth of its own clearly stood to lose as much as anyone from the nationalisation of private property. In Spain the Republican government of 1936 prepared to do just this to ecclesiastical property and the Spanish prelates, at least, were unequivocal in their support of Franco. The generals in return incorporated the Catholic faith in their right-wing ideology:

> Spaniards! Citizens of Burgos! [declared General Mola] The Government which was the wretched bastard of liberal and Socialist concubinage is dead, killed by our valiant army. Spain, the true Spain, has laid the dragon low, and now it lies, writhing on its belly and biting the dust. I am now going to take up my position at the head of the Troops and it will not be long before two banners—the sacred emblem of the Cross, and our own glorious flag—are waving together in Madrid (**65**).

The reader will form his own opinion of the quality of such rhetoric, but both the words and the sentiments expressed are those of the authentic reactionary right.

In Austria and in central and northern Europe generally, the local Catholic hierarchy gave its support to the political right only a fraction less overtly than in Spain. The Rumanian Fascists called themselves 'The Legion of the Archangel Michael'. The Belgians called themselves Rexists—followers of Christus Rex and, at the secular level, of the doctrines of Maurras. The Catholic party disowned them, however, and generally, in the more advanced areas of Europe, the link between the Church and the right was much weaker. The Vatican's Concordat with Mussolini was principally a tactical move of *realpolitik* and the German Catholic party's support for Hitler's Enabling Bill was a political mistake. Nazism was a movement which scored as many victories among protestants as among Catholics and was basically hostile to all organised religion not only because of its own *völkisch* ideology but also because of its intolerance of any authority within the state which might challenge its own. The evidence for and against the Church's connection with the political right is therefore equivocal and obscure.

'In origin,' Sir Oswald Mosley has written of Fascism, 'it was an explosion against intolerable conditions, against remediable wrongs which the old world had failed to remedy. It was a movement to

15

secure national reassurance by people who felt themselves threatened with decline into decadence and death and were determined to live, and live greatly' (**64**).

The latter part of this comment is the language of right-wing nationalism but the former is that of radicalism. Mosley is among those who have claimed Fascism for a force of the left, though not, of course, of the Communist left. Sir Oswald Mosley himself was the rising star of the British Labour Party until he was expelled for his radical Keynesian policies for the removal of unemployment and his outspoken criticism of the party leadership. The programme of the British Union of Fascists was radical: the abolition of political parties, though not of parliament, the organisation of a corporate state, schemes of public investment and public works, an attack on 'the rule of the financial gangster' and the development of the Empire as a self-sufficient economic unit. Perhaps because it never came near the achievement of power British Fascism retained its ideological purity, though by 1939 it had been largely diverted in practice into the ideological battle against Communism and tainted, in the eyes of the majority of the public, by its association with Hitler.

In this as in other respects British Fascism bore strong resemblances to Italian Fascism (**63**). Mussolini began his political career on the extreme of the anarchist left, and there is something of a mystery about the progress of the agitator who denounced both nationalism and the Church but became, in the course of time, their defender against the red menace of Communism (**49**). 'The Fatherland', said Mussolini at the time of the Libyan war of 1911–12, 'is a spook—like God, and like God it is vindictive, cruel and tyrannical. . . . Let us show that the Fatherland does not exist just as God does not exist' (**51**). In those early days the Vatican was 'that den of intolerance and a gang of robbers', and in his first postwar political programme the Fascist Mussolini proposed not only the confiscation of all ecclesiastical property, but also a progressive tax on capital and a tax of eight-five per cent on war profits, a minimum wage and workers' participation in the management of industrial enterprises. The germ of Anarcho-syndicalism remained in the Fascist Corporate State, which was the only genuine political innovation of Italian Fascism in power. The Corporations, composed of representatives of labour, capital and the government for every major occupation, 'guarantee judicial equality between employers and employed', claimed the Charter of Labour of 1927, 'and maintain the discipline of production and work and promote the improvement of both. The Corporations contribute the unified organization of the forces of production and represent completely the interests of production' (**21**). 'It is the State alone,' wrote Mussolini on another occasion, 'that can solve the dramatic contradictions of capitalism' [**doc. 6**].

As a solution to the social problems and divisions of society, the idea of the corporate state exercised the same attraction as the notion of a national unity which rose above the conflict of parties and subsumed it. It explains, to some extent, why Fascism won supporters among sections of the working-class and can be found in the Fascist ideologies both of France and of the Rumanian Cornelius Codreanu. In practice, Fascist anti-capitalism tended to degenerate into anti-semitism. Italy was an exception to this, since anti-semitism never played much part in Fascist ideology there and was in fact irrelevant in a country where there were very few Jews. In Italy, however, as elsewhere, in countries where an organised left existed, anti-capitalism tended in practice to give place to anti-Communism. Italian landowners and capitalists gave Fascism their financial support for this reason, and the chief characteristic of the Italian corporate state in action was not its restrictions on the activities of capitalists but its depression of wages and the abolition of the right to strike. It is for this reason that, in the final analysis, Fascism can be defined as a political phenomenon of the right.

In reaching this conclusion it is implied that the ideological slogans of Fascism may not have been entirely genuine. Either Mussolini did not mean what he said when he attacked the Church, nationalism and capitalism, or else he changed his mind, or perhaps he adopted the anti-Communist slogan as a matter of expediency when he saw, as in the parliamentary elections of 1919, that wherever his separate brand of Socialism might lead it would not bring him to power in competition with the organised left and the organised right and centre. This is where the mystery lies in defining his ideological position.

Walter Laqueur has suggested a similar inconsistency in Hitler's political thinking. In *Mein Kampf* Hitler equates Bolshevism with the international Jewish conspiracy, and in this correlation he found an unbeatable formula for political . success which transformed the extremist movement of the abortive Munich demonstration of 1923 into the mass party whose electoral successes brought him to power

17

ten years later. But before the Munich fiasco and the subsequent term of imprisonment which gave Hitler time to reflect upon the realities of politics and to write *Mein Kampf*, Laqueur points out, Hitler had been content to lambast the Socialist Republic for 'stabbing in the back' the undefeated German army and accepting the dictated treaty of Versailles, while anti-semitism had formed an equally passionate but separate theme. Laqueur suggests that the subsequent equation of Bolshevism with Judaism and their joint elevation to a leading place in Nazi propaganda may have been suggested to Hitler by some of his motley political associates of the early years. Alfred Rosenberg, author of the anti-semitic *Myth of the Twentieth Century* and Max von Scheubner-Richter were Baltic Germans, forced into exile by the advance of the Red Army. Along with their fellow-exiles, they brought to western Europe the forged *Protocols of Zion* which purported to reveal a Jewish conspiracy for world domination. In their already heated and wildly prejudiced minds, the rise of Russian Communism, some of whose leaders and whose ideological teacher, Karl Marx, were Jewish, seemed to manifest the crucial stage of the Jewish plot.

> From these quarters [Laqueur concludes] Hitler adopted the idea of anti-Bolshevism as a central plank in Nazi ideology and propaganda and equated Bolshevism with world Jewry. Whether and to what degree Hitler believed in all this (as Rosenberg and Scheubner-Richter, fanatical anti-Communists, undoubtedly did), and to what extent he merely regarded it as a useful myth in his domestic policy, and a good weapon in his foreign policy, is another question (**6**).

Laqueur's argument raises questions not only about the nature of the twentieth-century right but also about the basic qualities of political ideology itself. Is it possible that the Nazis and the Fascists themselves held mental reservations about the doctrines which they so fervently preached, manipulating themes and prejudices not only of the right but perhaps also of the left to no greater—or less—a purpose than the achievement of political power and the satisfaction of their own inadequate egos? If one result of this essay is to raise such questions in the reader's mind then it may not be a worthless purpose to have served. If the history of twentieth-century Europe teaches any lesson it is that the force of such prejudices and their expression in ideological form should never be underrated, and never, therefore, dismissed. To believe that Hitler did not mean what he said is a mistake that first the men of Munich and then Stalin made with fateful consequences. The fact that so many Germans did believe him is what gives ideological politics their fascination and their importance to the student of that history.

*Mein Kampf* is a remarkable book (**18**). Whatever the reader's reaction to its hysterical note and whatever mental reservations may or may not have lain in its author's mind, in its finished version and at inordinate and repetitive length, it links German nationalism, racialist myth, anti-semitism, social protest and anti-Communism into a consistent argument which follows logically from its wild premises. It also reveals a profound and intuitive understanding of the group psychology of mass politics and how its alarmingly crude emotions may be tapped and channelled.

'The instinct for the preservation of one's own species is the primary cause that leads to the formation of human communities,' Hitler wrote. 'Hence the State is a social organism and not an economic organisation' [**doc. 8**]. This is the fundamental premise of a political theory which rejected the theory of the class war but deplored social injustice because it seduced the working classes into the 'international camp' of Bolshevism. Like Maurras, Hitler held a *völkisch* concept of the German nation, which was a matter of blood, soil and culture. The German nation, truly conceived of, was a racial unity, the product of an historic struggle for self-preservation against rival but lesser races and the finest flower of Aryan civilisation. All the ills which had befallen Germany since 1914 could be traced to the failure of successive governments to realise that the racial question was the essence of the problems which faced them. The survival and recovery of Germany (and Germany, thus defined, included Hitler's homeland of Austria, the German settlements in the Baltic area and lands which Germans had acquired anywhere in Europe) was thus not a question of economics or even of military strength but of preserving the racial stock from corrupting influences [**doc. 8**].

What were these corrupting influences? The parliamentary democracy of the postwar Republic was clearly one, because it had sacrificed the German effort in the war and accepted the destruction of Germany in the peace of Versailles. Its party politicians divided the nation instead of uniting it. The capitalist system played a similar role. Beyond the evident shortcomings of the existing social and political system, however, lay a common root of corruption: the materialist obsession of modern society which diverted politicians from the racial question and seduced the masses into Marxism.

> What distinguished Karl Marx from the millions who were affected in the same way was that, in a world already in a state of gradual decomposition, he used his keen powers of prognosis to detect the essential poisons, so as to extract them and concentrate them, with the art of a necromancer, in a solution which would bring about the rapid destruction of the independent nations on the globe. But all this was done in the service of his race.
>
> Thus the Marxist doctrine is the concentrated extract of the mentality which underlies the general concept of life today ... the bourgeois world is permeated with all those same poisons and its conception of life in general differs from Marxism only in degree and in the character of the persons who hold it. The bourgeois world is Marxist but believes in the possibility of a certain group of people—that is to say, the bourgeoisie, being able to dominate the world, while Marxism itself systematically aims at delivering the world into the hands of the Jews.
>
> Over against all this, the *völkisch* concept of the world recognises that all the primordial racial elements are of the greatest significance for mankind (**18**) [**doc. 8**].

Closely allied to Hitler's detestation of materialism and Marxism was the anti-semitism which obtrudes in this quotation and which is perhaps the best known of all his ideological attributes. The foes of Aryanism, when all the disguises had been stripped away, were seen to be the Jews. The roots of Hitler's obsessive hatred for the Jews are the subject of speculation among his biographers. The sentiment was neither unique to him nor original (**53**). Anti-semitism in Europe is as old as Christianity itself but had reached a peak of intensity towards the end of the nineteenth century. The sociological reasons for this will be discussed in a later chapter. At the ideological level anti-semitism, along with the Aryan myth of which it was the counterpart, had entered European literature most noticeably with the publication in 1853 of Arthur de Gobineau's essay *On the Inequality of the Human Race*. Since then an undergrowth of racialist and anti-semitic literature had flowered which culminated in the publication in Russia just before the First World War, and the dissemination in Germany soon afterwards by white Russian and Baltic German refugees, of the forged *Protocols of Zion* which purported to disclose the historic plan of the Jewish race for the domination of Europe and the destruction of Christian civilisation. Generations of credulous readers had swallowed the myth of an Aryan master race, distinguished by such factors as its ancestry, its linguistic and its physical characteristics, waging or failing to wage a ceaseless battle against the Elders of the Sanhedrim who, according to one version, assembled every two hundred years by night in the Jewish cemetery at Prague to review the progress of their scheme.

Partly influenced by the study of language, partly by the Darwinian theory of natural selection, partly pure fantasy deriving from crude prejudice and a taste for macabre folklore, racist theory was the science fiction of the nineteenth and early twentieth centuries. When Hitler wrote that 'the world is not there to be dominated by the faint-hearted races' and 'in standing guard against the Jew I am defending the handiwork of the Lord' he spoke in a European tradition. While readers of history may feel incredulous amusement at the Nazi expedition to the Himalayas to look for the missing link in the racial chain or the plan for the establishment of a pure Aryan state in Burgundy, the realities of Hitler's 'final solution of the Jewish question' remain as a terrible example of the enormities of which this kind of ideological politics was capable.

A final characteristic of ideological politics, though it was to develop as fully on the left as on the right and provide yet another example of their similarity in practice, was the cult of the leader. His anti-semitism apart, probably the best known image of Hitler is of a diminutive figure held in the glare of searchlights and hailed by the massed ranks of the party members at a Nuremberg rally [**doc. 12**]. Mussolini is characteristically remembered on a Roman balcony before an adoring crowd and the veneration accorded to Stalin yields nothing in comparison.

How can the historian explain the domination of these figures over their contemporaries? The cult of hero-worship did not begin or end in early twentieth-century Europe, and the heroes of one generation usually seem vulgar charlatans to the next. In this period the cult of personality reached a peak of intensity, a climax which perhaps reflected the extent to which it was a work of art. The microphone, the radio and the film were the weapons of ideological propaganda which increased its pitch and extended its audience to unprecedented proportions. It was a willing audience, and the historian has still to explain why heroes were in such demand. Were they the twentieth-century's version of the divinely visited king, a European tradition which itself dates back to prehistoric magic? Were they answering the philosopher Nietzsche's call for a superman to emerge from the anonymous masses of industrialised and urban society to reimpose the mastery of individual man upon his over-powering material environment? Did they mark a resort by civilised man in a time of crisis to the primitive political organisation of the savage? Did the leaders themselves believe in their roles or was the cult of personality another example of propagandist manipulation of the masses? These questions are the subject of social psychology, and are also to some extent imponderable, since they denote a phenomenon which both pre-dated the twentieth century and still persists. It is a phenomenon which characterises the ideological parties in an essential way, and which emphasises once again their essentially primitive and irrational character.

No doubt the reader will have compared the ideologies of left and right reviewed in this and the previous chapter and formed his own opinion of their comparative merits and shortcomings. Some commentators have preferred the right, stressing the value of its insistence on tradition, continuity, patriotism and social cohesion by contrast with the divisiveness of the left and what Mosley calls its 'doctrine of modern disintegration' (**64**). Others have preferred the left, arguing that, with the exception of Anarchism and for all its criticisms of the character of industrial society, it nevertheless accepted the idea and the achievements of industrialism, urbanism and progress. The right, by contrast, was alien to such a society. It appealed to the fear of progress and the unknown, to the resentment of change, to what Hans Rogger calls 'an infantile yearning for protection (through nation, race, boundless power, or aimless activism) against dark and only dimly comprehended forces that lurk and threaten on all sides' (**47**).

The reader may prefer Anarchism, an idea which is not without a certain nobility and which has preserved it through having no history of the tainting experience of power. He may recoil altogether from the simplified rhetoric and brutal actions of ideological politics, which brought back to twentieth-century history the passion, the intolerance and the inhumanity of the religious wars of the seventeenth. If he does so he must accord at least a grudging respect to Hitler, whose grasp of the psychology of mass politics and of the technique of its manipulation history has proved to be correct, however depressing the picture it paints to the liberal and the intellectual mind:

> The broad masses of a nation are not made up of professors and diplomats. Since these masses have only a poor acquaintance with abstract ideas, their reactions lie more in the domain of the feelings, where the roots of their positive as well as their negative attitudes are explained. They are susceptible only to a manifestation of strength which comes either from the positive or negative side, but they are never susceptible to any half-hearted attitude that wavers between one pole and another. The emotional grounds of their attitude furnish the reason for their extraordinary stability. It is always more difficult to fight successfully against faith than against knowledge. Love is less subject to change than respect. Hatred is more lasting than mere aversion. And the driving force which has brought about the most tremendous revolutions on this earth has never been a body of scientific teaching which has gained power over the masses, but always a devotion which has inspired them, and often a kind of hysteria which has urged them to action.
>
> Whoever wishes to win over the masses must know the key that will open the door to their hearts. It is not objectivity, which is a feckless attitude, but a determined will, backed up by force when necessary (**18**) [**doc. 7**].

These concepts may not have been original to Hitler, but they provided the formula with which he built a mass movement and came to govern one of the most advanced and cultured societies of Europe. For all the 'scientific teaching' of Marxism these were also the methods its leaders used in their bid for power and its exercise where they achieved it. The following chapters will consider the successes and failures of left and right in action.

# Part Two

# THE PRACTICE

# 4 The Left in Action

'The whole of Europe is filled with the spirit of revolution,' wrote Lloyd George in 1919. 'There is a deep sense not only of discontent but of anger and revolt amongst the workmen against pre-war conditions. The whole existing order in its political, social and economic aspects is questioned by the masses of the population from one end of Europe to another' (**31**).

It was an alarming picture for the established orders of society and also a remarkable transformation. Although there was considerable overt working-class discontent, expressed in strikes and political demonstrations, on the eve of the first world war, the outbreak of war itself had reduced international Socialism to disarray as national parties put their country before the class struggle. War, however, in Trotsky's phrase, 'is the locomotive of history'. Without accepting the full determinist implications of his comment, it is clear that war is a critical test of the strength and cohesion of a society. When national security is at stake the immediate reflex is a heightened patriotism. This showed itself not only in Britain, France and Germany, but also in Tsarist Russia, where Nicholas II enjoyed a fleeting and unaccustomed popularity as the commander of his armies and the little father of his people. But as the strain of war begins to show itself in defeat, heavy casualties and economic restrictions, the ties of loyalty fray and threaten to snap. This happened in Germany right at the end of the war and in Russia in 1917 when, in the eye-witness opinion of Sir Robert Bruce-Lockhart: 'The revolution took place because the patience of the Russian people broke down under a system of unparalleled inefficiency and corruption.'

But for the war, the Russian revolution might conceivably never have occurred. When it did occur it was far from being exclusively socialist in its initial conception but rapidly became so.

What is important to realise [Bruce-Lockhart continued] is that from the first, the revolution was a revolution of the people. From

27

the first moment neither the Duma nor the intelligentsia had any control of the situation. Secondly, the revolution was a revolution for land, bread and peace—but above all for peace. There was only one way to save Russia from going Bolshevik. That was to allow her to make peace. It was because he would not make peace that Kerensky went under. It was solely because he promised to stop the war that Lenin came to the top.

What Lenin brought to the revolution when he alighted at the Finland Station were the qualities which have already been mentioned. These were the ideological conviction and determination that the revolution should take a Communist course, the disciplined support of a revolutionary organisation which had planned for such an event and the political judgment which could capitalise on a fluid but revolutionary situation. The discipline was not complete, because Bolshevik factions launched an attempted coup during the summer of 1917 which was against Lenin's advice and which resulted temporarily in his renewed exile. The political judgment was also daring and in those early days overlaid by ideological principles. Immediately upon his first arrival, Lenin demanded that

All power in the state, from top to bottom, from the remotest village to the last street in the city of Petrograd, must belong to the Soviets of Workers', Soldiers' and Peasants' Deputies. . . . There must be no police, no bureaucrats who have no responsibility to the people, who stand above the people; no standing army, only the people universally armed, united in the Soviets—it is they who must run the State [**doc. 4b**].

At the time when Lenin spoke, the Provisional Government still retained a measure of popular support for its policy of continuing the war. The Bolsheviks had only a small following among the peasants and controlled neither the Petrograd Soviet nor the All-Russian Congress of Soviets which met a month later. Events played into Lenin's hands, however, as power tends to flow to those who are prepared and organised to take it. As the summer passed with continuing defeats and desertions from the front and continuing shortages and political inaction at home, the Petrograd and Moscow masses were gradually radicalised. The July coup failed but the Tsarist general Kornilov's advance on Petrograd increased the general alarm and forced Kerensky to rehabilitate the Bolsheviks and rearm their Red Guards. In the autumn his coalition government collapsed and the Bolsheviks gained majority support within the Petrograd Soviet. Lenin judged that the moment had come. The government was at its weakest, the Bolsheviks in a momentary ascendancy which might end as soon as the second Congress of Soviets assembled, as it was due to do.

The immediate and almost bloodless success of the Bolshevik seizure of power confirmed his judgment. The Congress accepted the situation and the Constituent Assembly which met in January 1918 was dismissed at the point of a gun. The propaganda of peace, bread and land won popular support for the new rulers of Russia and the organisation and heroism of the party carried the new régime through the civil war that followed. The non-Marxist historian may truthfully point out that these events had little to do with the logic of history. The Communist revolution in Russia was a *coup d'état*. The principles which it did follow faithfully, however, were those of the technique of revolution which Lenin had developed and imposed upon his party in previous years and which he summed up, admittedly after the event, in *Left Wing Communism*:

> The art of politics (and the Communist's correct understanding of his task) lies in correctly gauging the conditions and the moment when the vanguard of the proletariat can successfully seize power, when it is able, during and after the seizure of power, to obtain adequate support from adequately broad strata of the working class and of the non-proletarian working masses, and when it is able thereafter to maintain, consolidate and extend its rule by educating, training and attracting ever broader masses of the working people (**11**).

Even Lenin had confidently expected that the Russian revolution would be followed by a chain of revolutions across the continent. Communist risings took place in Vienna and Berlin, and Soviet régimes took power briefly in Budapest, Munich and some areas of northern Italy. None of these achievements proved more than ephemeral. The reasons for their failure are several, but combine to show that history takes its own course rather than following the dictates of ideology (**6, 35**).

The first of these reasons was the factor which had divided European Socialists before the first world war and continued to divide them and which has been noted already in chapter 2. It was that there was an enormous variation among the social and political structures of the countries of the continent. This variation made the situation in backward Russia almost unique in the opportunities it offered for left-wing revolution. It had two important effects. The first was that governments were much less likely to be overthrown if they had existed long and successfully enough to retain the support of a majority of the people. If this was so then even the most adverse economic circumstances—and these were present over most of the continent in the forms of inflation and unemployment—could prove insufficient to break them, and if they were broken the basic political structure might remain in its former state. The second was that in many countries, particularly in western Europe, the socialist left had deeper roots and was more closely attached to the existing political system than was the case in Russia. This was demonstrated in Britain, for instance, where there were many postwar strikes and effective demonstrations against the government's policy of active intervention against the Bolsheviks, but where the trade union movement as a whole held aloof from any kind of revolutionary action and was drawn most reluctantly into the subsequent fiasco of the General Strike. On the political front, the Labour Party not only refused to adopt a revolutionary ideology, but also refused affiliation to the newly formed Communist Party of Great Britain, which from then on was consigned to the fringe of political activity (**41**).

The differences between Russia and western Europe were most spectacularly defined in Germany; here postwar events bore at first a striking resemblance to those recently witnessed in Russia. The monarchy fell, to be succeeded by an uneasy provisional government. The economic situation of the working class was in places desperate through food shortages. An All-German Congress of Workers' and Soldiers' Councils assembled, and the fact that the revolutionary Marxists were only a minority within it while the majority opted to summon a constituent assembly and create a parliamentary republic seemed to enthusiasts only to provide one more parallel with the Bolshevik experience. They rejected the decision of the majority Socialists to endorse the new constitution and formed the German Communist Party in December 1918. When half the provisional government resigned the Communists took to the streets, where they were shot down by units of the regular army and the theoretically illegal *Freikorps*, a volunteer force of ex-officers whom the government were prepared to use in the emergency. The leaders Karl Liebknecht and Rosa Luxemburg were murdered. Rosa Luxemburg had been dubious of the chances of success from the start. Like the Bolshevik observer Karl Radek, she believed that 'the seizure of political power can be affected only by a majority of the working class, which in January was certainly not on the side of the Communist Party' (**31, 38**) [**doc. 10a**]. In fact, the German working class followed the leaders of the Social Democratic party, who themselves remained loyal to constitutional political methods. In doing so they certainly reflected the attitude of the German bourgeoisie, a class much more socially and politically significant than its stunted counterpart in Russia, and they also held, if only temporarily and with many reservations, the support of the military high command, which in general maintained its authority through the crisis and thus continued to play its historically powerful role in German politics.

The history of the German Communist Party did not end in 1919, and continues to be instructive to a study of the European left in action. Still guided by the Russian situation, the Communists regarded the Kapp Putsch of 1920, which the government survived because of a general strike of its loyal trade union supporters, as Germany's Kornilov coup. Their earlier failure they now classified as the 'July Days' of German Bolshevism and proceeded to a new wave of strikes and riots in 1921. On this occasion they were resisted by the mass of workers, who preferred to keep their jobs, and broken and arrested by the police and the military. The membership of the German Communist Party is said to have declined by as much as three-fifths after this fiasco.

During the economic crisis of 1928 to 1932, Communist votes ran into several millions. They failed again to achieve power for reasons which will be considered shortly. The comparison of their popularity with the situation a few years before draws attention to a continuing basic weakness. The Communists had no broad-based continuing strength, either in voting support or in party membership. As late as 1933, when Hitler was beginning to exert the full power of the state in a counter-attack from the right, the Social Democrats maintained a loyal bloc of seven million votes. Communist votes seem to have come from the unemployed, from the least politically sophisticated members of the working class, even perhaps like the Nazis from those who had never concerned themselves with voting before. Analysis of party membership produces a similar picture. Only a small minority represented skilled workers or stayed long. The majority were unemployed and young rather than old. Communism in Germany, Neil McInnes concludes, drew fleeting support from transient social categories. It never enjoyed permanent support and never threatened to oust the moderate Social Democrats as the leading party of the left (**35**).

Shifting and impermanent though it was, there was some support for Communism in Germany between 1928 and 1932. Another factor in its failure to launch a successful revolution during these years was its defective political judgment. In 1919 and in 1921 the party had been over-confident. During the second economic and political crisis of the postwar period it was complacent. The levels of unemployment and of political discontent were such that the Communists seem to have believed that the revolution would occur this time almost without their intervention. Certainly their tactics were totally misguided. They virtually ignored the political rise of Hitler and concentrated their efforts on disrupting the Socialist struggle to maintain democratic government. In 1932, when the Social Democratic government of Prussia was deposed by military action on the instructions of Hindenburg's presidential government, the Communists assisted its destruction. In the autumn of the same year a strike of Berlin transport workers broke out, led by the Communists and undertaken against the advice of the trade unions. The Nazis joined in to attack blacklegs and police. It was an incongruous alliance and cost the Nazis seats in the ensuing elections. The Communists gained some working class support but every step they took towards destroying the existing system of government played into the hands of its eventual heirs, the Nazi party (**6, 35**).

Why did the Communists underrate their Nazi opponents? Almost certainly because, since Hitler's propaganda could not be reduced to the category of a class ideology, they failed to understand the forces which he represented. The Communists were more concerned with the power of 'social Fascism' as they described the Social Democratic party. Hitler seemed to them, if anything, an extreme exponent of its ideology. 'The bourgeoisie won't let Hitler anywhere near power. Let's go to Lichtenberg and play skittles,' said the Communist leader Thaelmann on the day before Hitler was made Chancellor of the Reich (**6**).

The German Communists were blinkered by their ideological preconceptions. In this they were not alone on the Communist left. It was Stalin who had defined parliamentary Socialism as social

Fascism [**doc. 10b**] and in repeating his error, the Communists were showing themselves loyal members of the international Communist movement. The Third, or Communist International, was founded in 1919 when the postwar revolutionary fervour of the left was at its height. Such was the intoxication of those days that it detached substantial fractions from the existing Socialist parties of Germany, Italy and western Europe. It met in Moscow, the natural and indeed the only possible venue, since it was in Russia alone that Socialist revolution had been able to establish and maintain itself. It was also natural for the same reasons to look to Lenin and the Russian party for ideological and tactical leadership. Even at this early stage some delegates grumbled at the insistence of the Russian comrades that their view of tactics must prevail regardless of differing national political and social circumstances. Lenin, as always, stood for discipline and the correctness of his own views of the moment. No less than twenty-one conditions of membership were attached to Comintern and, in practice, they amounted to a single effect: the supremacy of the Moscow party line (**31, 34, 35, 37**) [**doc. 10b**].

The Moscow party line was intimately connected with the security of the Russian revolution, then under the most serious attack of the Whites and their interventionist allies. It was Moscow's interest to forment revolution everywhere, if only to distract the attention of hostile capitalist governments from the Russian Civil War. The ill-fated German Communist risings were influenced by this policy. In 1921 the war ended. At home Lenin embarked upon the compromises of the New Economic Policy and abroad he looked for a re-opening of Russian commerce. Revolutionaries were an embarrassment to such a policy, which was one of the considerations behind Lenin's denunciation of 'left-wing' Communism as an 'infantile delusion'. Correct tactics now were redefined as a policy of cooperation with the moderate Socialist and trade union movement: 'The whole task of the Communists is to be able to *convince* the backward elements, to work *among* them, and not to *fence themselves off* from them by artificial and childishly "Left" slogans' (**11**).

In the face of the abject failure of European Communists either to win revolutions or even the leadership of the left this was sound advice whatever the motives behind it. A few years later, however, Stalin altered the party line again, demanding a return to ultra-left tactics and a separation from non-Communist elements. Deutscher (**36**) suggests that this change of mind sprang from Stalin's own struggle with the moderates within the Russian party in which he could strengthen his own position by an appeal to the international movement, or even from Chiang Kai Shek's purge of Communists from the Kuomintang which led Stalin to conclude that Social Democrats could not be trusted as allies. Whatever the reason Social Democrats now became 'social Fascists' and the German party, along with others, obediently switched to its mutually destructive attack on them. The party line changed again, in the thirties, to the united front against Fascism. By this time, however, it was too late to save the German party from destruction at Hitler's hands.

Whether a united front could have saved German Socialism is dubious, however. The combined vote of the Social Democrats and the Communists at their zenith was never more than 40·4 per cent of the total cast in the critical elections which preceded the Nazi accession to power. The final reason for the failure of the left was the strength and success of the right in action. In that success the Comintern-dictated tactics of the German party inflicted a two-edged fatal blow. The Communists weakened the left and also discredited it. To the frightened right, the subtleties of the party line and its ideological formulations were either unknown or insignificant. Revolutionary Socialism was the spectre which haunted their imagination and in such a mood there was little to choose between parliamentary Socialists and Communists. The Nazi propaganda fed on this emotional confusion. It was the same everywhere in Europe. Even in Britain, of all European countries the least affected by the ideological battle of the interwar years, the 'Red smear' of the Zinoviev Letter was a potent factor in the defeat of Labour in the election of 1924, principally, perhaps, because it drove previously Liberal voters to the right.

The failures of Socialism in power belong in a later chapter. In concluding this one it may be said that the Bolshevik victory in Russia was a curiously and ironically mixed blessing to the course of the European left. It was a tremendous inspiration, because it demonstrated that theory could become fact. Beyond that it proved an often fatal hindrance. It led the more volatile elements of the left to conclude that what had succeeded in Russia must succeed elsewhere. It elevated ideological dreams to a place in the revolutionary consciousness above the consideration of the facts of political life. The supremacy which the Russian Communist party established reinforced this tendency and weakened both Communism and the non-Communist left. Above all, perhaps, the Bolshevik revolution inspired fear throughout Europe. In the remarks of Lloyd George with which this chapter opened, the reader may detect a note of sympathy for the aspirations of the left. If so, this was not a common reaction. The triumph of Bolshevism not only caused the spectre of Communism to walk again but clothed the phantom in flesh and blood. In doing so it provided the propagandist inspiration of the twentieth-century right.

# 5 The Right in Action

The first world war marks the beginning of Fascism as clearly as it does the emergence of modern Communism. Quite apart from its crucial contribution to the Bolshevik revolution, it raised nationalist emotions to unprecedented heights and then left them, suspended and frustrated, in the limbo of postwar disappointment and depression. It destroyed, perhaps permanently, the stability of economic and therefore of social life. During the war most governments abandoned the gold standard as the basis of national currency in face of the need to finance the war effort. An insistent inflation then began which became critically evident during the shortages of the postwar depression in international trade. The world economic crisis of 1929–32 can be traced to the same developments. Inflation is for the middle class what unemployment is for the workers. It reduces the value of fixed incomes and at its worst makes savings worthless. It can make the solid bourgeois, traditionally the most loyal supporter of established government, a discontented radical, though his radicalism is more likely to veer to the right than to the left.

The war also had radical psychological effects on individuals. Statesmen looked for a return to normalcy, but for young men everything seemed possible in a world turned upside down and from which so many of the middle generation had vanished. Ex-soldiers found civilian life ungrateful and disappointing. The radical right offered many of them comradeship, action and a cause. Mussolini's Fascist Squads, the German Free Corps, the Austrian *Heimwehr* and the French *Croix de Feu* of Colonel Casimir de la Roque are a few examples of this trend.

Mussolini was the first to unite all these elements in a political force. Italy had ended the war on the winning side but had few trophies of victory to show for it. The war had excited Mussolini's volatile mind and he had become one of the loudest of the interventionists who drove the country to participate in it. The result had been a bitter breach with the non-interventionist Socialist party which Mussolini did not forgive for his expulsion. He was now a wouldbe leader without a following, but personnel and issues lay at hand. D'Annunzio's march on Fiume at the head of squads of ex-servicemen inspired Mussolini to a renewed nationalism and to the formation of the *Fasci di combattimento*. But who were they to fight? There was ample material for revolution in postwar economic conditions in Italy, where prices doubled in the two years after the war and unemployment was rife. Mussolini's attempt to gain a following on the left in postwar elections failed. The working class stayed loyal to the Socialist party, which itself was in the process of splitting over the question of adherence to Comintern, or, in the Anarchist tradition, spontaneously and locally seized control of factories and rural estates. Mussolini, by the rapid and mysterious conversion which has already been noted, decided to fight the militant left (**46, 49**).

He found almost immediately the support which had previously eluded him. In two years, more than two thousand Fascist Squads were formed and proceeded to attack the red communes and collectives in transport supplied by landowners and paid for by capitalists. Weapons were supplied by the regular army. In 1920 the Minister of War offered four-fifths of their former pay to ex-officers who joined the Fascists. In the general election of 1921 Fascism became a popular political force, securing thirty-five seats in an electoral alliance with the veteran centrist prime minister Giolitti.

Giolitti, along with other parliamentary statesmen of his own and other nations, seems to have reasoned that Fascism would be harnessed if it was admitted to power. In his case, as in most of the others, this proved a miscalculation. The Italian Fascist technique became the classical ploy of the lawless right. It exploited political violence in the manner first advocated by Sorel, creating a disorder which itself alone could quell simply by withdrawing its forces. In 1922 the Fascists smashed Socialism when they broke a general strike with atrocious violence, and then turned their columns on Rome itself. The march on Rome brought Mussolini to power in a coalition government of the anti-left.

Many historians have commented both on the smallness and poor equipment of these columns and on the incongruous figure of their hero, who arrived to meet the king by train from Milan, in a black shirt and a bowler hat. Perhaps Italian Fascism began and even continued as a bluff and perhaps Mussolini never wanted to become a dictator. It was a brilliant bluff, however, which played on the fears and prejudices of the established orders of Italian society to bring the first Fascists to power. Reviewing their rise and noting the people who supported them, the student must classify it as one of the first totally successful counterrevolutions of the right. Its only rival to an exclusive claim to this title is the régime of Admiral Horthy in Hungary, which was established as a regency in 1919 after Romanian troops, acting on the orders of the Entente Powers, had destroyed the brief Soviet régime in Budapest. Some features of the Horthy régime may be claimed to confer on it a more exclusive claim to the title of a right-wing movement. It was overtly Christian, supported by the prelates of the Church as a force for moral restoration against the forces both of Liberalism and Marxism, and ferociously anti-semitic both in words and actions. It was also fiercely nationalistic, playing on the disappointments of Hungarians who had hoped for much more from the ruin of the Dual Monarchy than they obtained from the Treaty of Trianon. Above all it was anti-Bolshevik, and found its most fertile inspiration in its account of the horrors of the régime of Bela Kun in Budapest. The origin of the Hungarian right, as of the Italian, lay in the challenge from the left. In the years which followed, it revealed a lack of positive policies which exceeded that of Italy by far. Perhaps it was truly, therefore, the more purely reactionary of the two régimes. On the other hand, to emphasise the inconsistencies of European politics in this period, it maintained a front of parliamentary elections, which Italian Fascism soon dispensed with as it tightened its grip on power (**47, 67**).

The march on Rome inspired Hitler's Munich rising of 1923. This also was intended to develop into a march on Berlin and the complete overthrow of the Socialist government which Hitler detested as much for nationalist as for other ideological reasons. Like the German Communists, Hitler had on this occasion miscalculated. The heady oratory of beer-cellar politics and the presence at his side of the wooden hero Ludendorff had deluded him into thinking that the hysterical emotions of his circle were those of Germany at large. In reality, they were not even those of Bavaria at the time. Despite the inflationary crisis of 1923 and despite, or perhaps because of, the shortlived experience of Kurt Eisner's Munich Soviet of 1919, or perhaps because the state authorities nurtured their own plans for a political coup, Hitler's demonstration was dispersed. It had long-term effects. When, a few years later, a second economic crisis gnawed at the foundations of German society and politics, Hitler was a figure nationally known to discontented voters. He himself had spent the interim period in a way characteristic of Lenin, reflecting on the lessons of failure, extending party organisation and stiffening discipline, and collecting and deploying new slogans with which to broaden and deepen the party's appeal.

The series of events which finally brought Hitler to power is both too complex and probably too well known to the reader to merit detailed repetition in an essay of this length (54). The economic crisis precipitated a political crisis in which the coalition government led by the Social Democrats collapsed. Nazi and Communist street violence increased, and so did their respective voting strengths. No new coalition could be formed, so President Hindenburg, under the terms of the Weimar constitution, ruled by special decree. His first appointee as chancellor, the Catholic Centrist Brüning, failed either to halt the economic slide or to stem the tide of extremism. He was dismissed in favour of the Nationalist aristocrat von Papen. In a complex process of intrigue the soldier von Schleicher temporarily displaced von Papen until the situation was finally resolved, in January 1933, by the formation of a Nationalist-Nazi bloc and the appointment of Hitler as chancellor. His position was rapidly confirmed in the elections which followed the Reichstag fire. The Nazis gained 44 per cent of votes cast—more than the combined showing of the left—and the Nationalists 8 per cent. The Nazification of the Reich began.

The historical controversy which surrounds these events derives from the question of responsibility for Hitler's rise to power (57). An impersonal explanation is possible. As in France, a system of proportional representation encouraged the formation of a multitude of parties and imposed no need for moderation or responsibility upon them. Had not Germany been condemned to government by coalition, the crisis might never have arisen or might have been survived. For ideological historians, as for its ideological contemporaries, such an impersonal explanation of the fall of the German Republic is inadequate. They demand villains. For the left these are the members of the capitalist-military-aristocratic gang whose intrigues around Hindenburg resulted in Hitler's adoption. For the right, mass democracy itself is sometimes held to blame, since the rise of a demagogue is not possible except in a democratic constitution. Both points of view clearly contain elements of truth though, as is

D

usual in ideological discussions, they are exaggerated and over-simplified. It was intrigue which put Hitler in office, the intrigue of a ruling class which had never willingly accepted the installation of the democratic Republic and which was not sorry to see it fall and Socialism destroyed. On the other hand, these men would never have made use of Hitler for the purpose, or even have been able to achieve their purpose, had he not been the leader of a powerful political force within the existing system. The Nationalists needed Hitler's votes. German capitalists, Laqueur has shown, were few and cautious in their support of Hitler right up to the moment of his installation in power. It was his share—44 per cent—of the popular democratic vote which made Hitler a candidate for power. It may be added that the Communists, by abetting the rise of violence and the fall of the Social Democratic government of Prussia, made their own powerful contribution to the final result. The concluding question remains—who voted for Hitler?

Not surprisingly, this subject is hardly less controversial than any so far considered. No one wants to take the blame for Nazism, either in Germany or in Europe at large or to be regarded as the sort of person who might have supported the party had he been alive and present at the time. In summary the evidence seems by now fairly clear. Some members of the working class were Nazis in the critical period, not least the unemployed, and some of the officer caste, but analysis of the voting shows that neither the Social Democrats nor the Nationalists nor the Catholic Centre party lost much support in the critical elections. The mass of smaller parties which represented small farmers and professional and self-employed men in little provincial towns did. Some historians have postulated that the Nazi voters were men and women who had never voted before. It seems reasonable, however, to conclude that many of them must have come from the ranks of the Protestant and provincial petty bourgeoisie (5).

This general conclusion receives striking support in detail from William Sheridan Allen's study of the rise of Nazism in fictionally named Thalburg, a small town near Hanover (55). Here the Nazis emerged as a mass party between 1928 and 1933, finally claiming almost two out of every three votes cast in the Reichstag election carried out when Hitler was chancellor. Some of these votes could conceivably have come from a minor erosion of Nationalist or Social Democratic support, some came, so to speak, from nowhere, but the two parties which virtually disappeared from the electoral scene were the regional Hanoverian party and the petty bourgeois People's Party. Passing on from statistics to a study of Thalburg's political behaviour, Allen concludes that three factors may be cited to account for the rising crescendo of Nazi popularity. The first was a demand for German greatness which acted 'as if World War I had never ended'. The second was the economic crisis which, though it did not destroy the burgher's livelihood, made them 'desperate with fear'. The third, linked with this, was a fear of social revolution in which Communists and Social Democrats became indistinguishable.

Hitler had showed a keen insight into the hopes and fears of this social class in *Mein Kampf*:

> The ditch which separates that class, which is by no means economically well-off, from the manual labouring class is often deeper than people think. The reason for this division, which we may almost call enmity, lies in the fear that dominates a social group, which has only just risen above the level of the manual labourer—a fear lest it may fall back into its old conditions or at least be classed with the labourers. Moreover, there is something repulsive in remembering the cultural indigence of that lower class and their rough manner with one another; so that people who are only on the first rung of the social ladder find it unbearable to be forced to have any contact with the cultural level and standard of living out of which they have passed. . . . In the case of such a person, the hard struggle through which he passes often destroys his normal sympathy. His own fight for existence kills his sensibility for the misery of those who have been left behind (**18**).

This is a much subtler analysis of an advanced society than anything the Communists achieved. Taken with Allen's findings it also emphasises that Nazism was a force of the right. It made vague promises of national greatness and moral restoration, and, in later years, some positive effort to guarantee farm prices and produce a people's motor-car. Essentially, however, it appealed to a negative anti-Socialism, and on that its electoral success was built. The middle class, of course, has a right to its dreams and fears as inviolable as that of the workers or the rich. For historical purposes what must be distinguished is that it played as crucial a role as capitalism or Communism in the ideological transformation of twentieth-century politics.

The same balance of social forces can be observed in the politics of

Austria and central Europe. Eugen Weber, in his study of Fascism in Rumania (**7, 47**) distinguishes the same support among the middle orders of society though this occurred in a much less advanced economy and extended down to some levels of the working class in the absence of a powerful Communist or other left challenge. Anti-semitism provided the cement of the right in such areas. It carried over into Austria, Hungary and Germany as well, of course. The peculiar, historical social position of the Jews in Europe, excluded as they were from landowning and government service over most of the continent, had virtually forced them into business and the professions. Once in they prospered and at many critical points in economic life appeared to compete with, to block the path of, or to exploit, the petty bourgeoisie. In Vienna and Berlin they figured prominently in the professions, the press, the arts and entertainment world which the right fervently detested on moral grounds, and in the department store business. In smaller communities, less industrialised and urbanised, they were the entrepreneurs of small-scale capitalism: shopkeepers and moneylenders, farm stewards and middlemen in the milling and lumber industries. In the more backward parts of Europe they retained their exclusiveness to a more traditional degree, wearing time-honoured costumes and hair styles and continuing to speak Yiddish. Everywhere they provided a natural focus for social resentments which looked for a recognisably human explanation of the predicament. They were an irresistibly attractive target for the ideological propaganda of the right. In postwar Europe some Communist governments appear to have shared or exploited the same convenient sentiments.

Weber has also studied the supporters of *Action française* and the picture which emerges bears strong similarities to that found elsewhere (**62**). They were *rentiers*, small property-owners and farmers, shopkeepers and white-collar workers, schoolmasters and doctors, 'la classe des moyennes et petites gens de France', threatened by inflation, the big capitalism of the 'two hundred families' who were alleged to control the French economy, and also by the fear of social revolution. Georges Valois left them, disgusted at their negative lack of dynamism, to found the French Fascist movement properly so-called. René Doriot, political boss of St Denis, similarly quit the French Communist Party to found the *Parti populaire française* (**7**) These two defections, the one from the right and the other from the left, are sometimes taken to emphasise the dynamic nature of

Fascism in its more positive form, though they amounted to little enough in practice and Doriot ended, like Maurras, as a collaborator with the Nazis. What their failure also emphasises is the failure of political extremism in France. Although its constitution contained all the weaknesses and invitations to reckless extremism which have already been established, and although its political divisions may have contributed to the fall of France in 1940, there was no capitulation to extremism between the wars.

The possible reasons for this present an intriguing but imprecise picture. The French Communist Party was the largest in western Europe with a support which extended across Parisian factory-workers to peasant farmers. It was a faithful follower of the Moscow line, a fact which precipitated Doriot's angry breach with it because it maintained the doctrine of ultra-leftism at a time when this seemed only to condemn it to powerlessness. When the right emerged into the streets of Paris in 1934 and 1935, denouncing in Maurrassian terms the republican scandal of the Stavisky affair and threatening violence to democratic government, the Communist response, admittedly guided by the new anti-Fascist Stalinist tactic, was to form a Popular Front with the Socialists and Radicals, which came briefly to power in 1936. The French Communists have continued to disappoint the radicals to the left. Their resistance to Nazi occupation yielded nothing in heroism to that of others and the strike power which they wield through trades unions is formidable. In 1968, however, as on earlier occasions, they declined to assist in the overthrow of the existing system of government, perhaps fearing what might take its place.

Analysis shows that the leadership of the French Communist Party has always been old. Indeed in the period between the wars leadership was old in every aspect of French life just because the population as a whole was old rather than young. Perhaps therefore it was gerontocracy both on the left and on the right which saved democracy in France, just as France looked to the veterans Pétain and de Gaulle when crisis became overpowering. As has already been said, the relative failure of extremism in France is a puzzling phenomenon. Extremism was less successful there than elsewhere. Anglo-Saxons too often tend to ignore this in their over-simplified thinking about French society and politics. It points the historian's attention back to a consideration which has several times been made in this essay: that the success or failure of political extremism, like the character of left and right ideology, is modified by the prevailing political and social system (**40, 47**).

This is nowhere demonstrated more clearly than in the history of Britain itself. Britain experienced unemployment and inflation in this period and, despite the structure of its electoral system, the uncertainties of coalition government on more than one occasion. It produced a Communist party and the British Union of Fascists. Sir Oswald Mosley, the rising star of the Labour party in the twenties, formed the Union after the Labour party had expelled him for his radical Keynesian suggestions for the solution of economic problems and his outspoken criticism of its own timid orthodoxy in these matters. Like Mussolini he decided, after the ignominious electoral defeat of his New Party, to appeal to a broader following by more dramatic methods. Like Mussolini in his basic thinking, he proposed a radical reformation of the existing political and economic system the salient features of which have been described in an earlier chapter. Like Mussolini however, Mosley put his followers in black shirts and became increasingly concerned with the Communist threat. He was accused of anti-semitism. His demonstrations ended in street violence, at Olympia in 1934 and in Cable Street in 1936. The reaction of the ruling great coalition of Conservative, National Liberal and National Labour parties was decisively different from that of the Italian government, chiefly because it was based on the confidence of mass public support. The uniforms and the demonstrations were banned and Fascism declined. The growing tensions in Europe and the outbreak of the war finished it as a political force (**63, 64**).

The example of Spain, where the fortunes of the right were dramatically different, may more conveniently be considered in a later chapter. The example of Britain serves well to underline this chapter's conclusions as to the record of the right and action. These conclusions echo those drawn from an examination of the left. In the disturbed social conditions of Europe after the first world war, when certainties dissolved and problems seemed beyond the competence of parliamentary governments to solve, there was abundant material for the construction of a non-Communist political radicalism as well as for proletarian revolution itself. The non-Communist extremists could be equally radical, at least in theory, in their criticism and condemnation of the existing state of affairs. It was their anti-Communism which distinguished them in common from the left. This anti-Communism, whatever its motives, was their most potent slogan in winning support in every class of society, but particularly among those who felt most threatened by the processes of change and dissolution—the middle class crushed between the upper and nether millstones of capitalism and social revolution, but particularly fearful of the monster from the depths. Sociologists like Seymour Lipset distinguish between a Fascism of the right, exemplified in Spain and to some extent in Italy, and that of the centre describing its support in Germany (5). In ideological terms, however, the distinguishing characteristic of Fascism and Nazism was that it was anti-left, and to this it could attribute most of its successes in achieving power.

As for the left, achievement of power for the right was a matter of political circumstances and political judgment. If a pre-existing system or pre-existing loyalties were deeply rooted, as in Britain or, by the look of it, in France, success was not to be achieved. In Italy and in Germany the system was weaker and elsewhere almost non-existent, but its overthrow nevertheless depended on a mixture of qualities which the successful candidate for the succession must deploy. These had been catalogued by Hitler as they were by Lenin. They included organisation and discipline, skilful and insistent propaganda, shrewd judgment of the moment to strike and, finally, the ruthless use of political violence to sweep away resistance. Because these recipes for success were so similar, it is perhaps less than surprising that the left and the right behaved so similarly in power.

# 6 The Left in Power

Pride of place in any account of the left in power must go to Communist Russia. It provided the unique example in the period before the second world war of a radically left régime which succeeded in consolidating and maintaining its authority and in engineering a social revolution, even though the extent and effects of that revolution were less profound than ideology had envisaged.

The 'dictatorship of the proletariat', as has already been mentioned, was among the least defined of Marxist terms. In an equally famous phrase, Engels referred to the 'withering away of the state'. The proletariat would need to exercise state power to establish its class domination over the last pockets of feudalism and capitalism. As the classless society became established the state, as the organisation of the ruling class, would cease to fulfil a historical function and thus lose its reason to exist.

These were the postulates of theoretical Marxism. When Lenin wrote *State and Revolution* (**10**) on the eve of the Bolshevik seizure of power in 1917, the problem was a practical one. Lenin, as might be expected from what has already been established about his cast of mind, approached it in a pre-eminently pragmatic way while taking care to reconcile the demands of tactics with the phrases of the classical ideology. He made no promises about the speed of the process of transition from a class-based to a classless society but concentrated on the necessity for the Bolsheviks to retain state power if they were to influence the future development of sprawling, backward and, outside Petrograd and Moscow, still largely hostile Russia. He fully realised that in a democratic, parliamentary régime such as the other left parties advocated, the Bolsheviks would be overridden. At the level of ideological argument, therefore, the dictatorship of the proletariat now became 'the very essence of Marx's teaching' and the true Marxist 'one who *extends* the acceptance of class struggle to the acceptance of the dictatorship'. At the practical level the dictatorship of the proletariat became the dictatorship of the

Bolshevik party. It was an entirely consistent development from Lenin's theory of the disciplined organisation of revolutionaries [**doc. 4b**].

Nevertheless Lenin said and seems to have intended that such a dictatorship should be less repressive and more democratic than the Tsarist system which it replaced. Events imposed a different pattern. For almost four years after 1917 the Bolsheviks were confronted by a desperate civil war in which both whites and Social Revolutionaries disputed their control of Russia, and the states of western Europe actively intervened to arrest the overthrow of Bolshevism. There was widespread famine, and industrial production fell away catastrophically. In such a situation strong government was essential to the survival of the régime. Only loyal party members could safely be trusted with authority. Only loyal party members indeed could be relied on to face the dangers, the unpopularity and the privations which the situation imposed. Thus Trotsky despatched political commissars to join the units of the Red Army and prevent their defection to the enemy. Party representatives went into the countryside to seize grain from the hostile farmers and into the factories to stimulate production. Party members formed and led the *Cheka*, a political police force which instituted a 'Red Terror' against known and suspected enemies of the régime after an attempt on Lenin's life in 1918.

The heroism of these members, and their ruthlessness, saved the revolution and vindicated both Lenin's theory of party organisation and his interpretation of proletarian dictatorship. If the party had not insisted on such total power some of these extremities might never have been reached. Once the civil war ended there was a widespread reaction against the claims and methods of the Communists, symbolised by the mutiny of the Kronstadt naval garrison in March 1921 and demands for 'Communism without the Bolsheviks'. Like the Jacobins before them, the Bolsheviks had survived the counter-revolution of the *emigrés* and the Vendéans only to be confronted by the threat of a new Thermidor. The failure of Communist revolutions everywhere else in Europe added to their isolation. Lenin's response was a shift of tactics to concession. Just as the policy of Comintern changed from hard-line revolutionism to cooperation with other parties of the left, in Russia Lenin instituted the New Economic Policy, inviting the cooperation not only of the other parties of the Russian left but also of the farmers and industrialists by a return to some measure of private enterprise in an effort to restore the shattered economy.

Historians sometimes ask what might have happened in Russia had Lenin lived beyond 1924. Might N.E.P. have been extended and developed into an evolutionary type of Communism quite different from the grim totalitarianism which came to characterise Stalin's régime? Like all such historical questions, this one is unanswerable. It is true that Lenin warned the party against Stalin's taste for personal power, but even while Lenin lived, the party was re-establishing and extending its power behind the front of N.E.P. In the early twenties, opposing parties were banned and liquidated along with opposing factions within the Communist party itself. The trade unions were reorganised and subjected to political control. The political police remained actively in existence. It is a reasonable argument, therefore, to maintain that the policy of the Communists developed consistently from what it had been to what it became and remains: an organisation demanding total internal loyalty and total external power. Anything else is a change of tactics. The true believer will dispute this, but even his faith may be taken to demonstrate the power of ideological slogans and party discipline over the mind.

The same questions recur when Stalinism is considered (**32, 33, 34**) [**doc. 10c**]. The long period of Stalinist rule in Russia presents two aspects. The first is of a massive and successful effort to feed, employ and modernise Russia—in Marxist words, 'to increase the total of productive forces as rapidly as possible'. It must also be added that Stalinism raised literacy and social services to an unprecedented level within the Soviet Union. Western commentators sometimes ignore the positive achievements of Russian Communism which gave it a claim to popular loyalty independent of ideology and party totalitarianism. Nevertheless, the second feature of Stalinism is totalitarianism: censorship and police repression, forced labour and political imprisonment. What, if any, is the connection between the two? It can be argued that the policies of oppression were forced upon Stalin by the exigencies of the situation. Industry could not develop quickly except under pressure and could not develop at all marooned in a peasant economy which would willingly produce neither food nor manpower for the cities. Freedom to prosper while millions starved might indeed seem indefensible and freedom to criticise while the states of western Europe hoped daily for the collapse of the first

Socialist state might seem a dangerous luxury. It can also be argued that Russia during this period experienced changes no more nor less traumatic than those which accompanied the industrial revolution in western Europe, or that even at his worst, Stalin was no more than the last of the Tsars, faced with the classic problems of Peter the Great and copying his means of coping with them.

On the other hand, Marxist-Leninism had promised a new historical experience, a social development free from the wretched conditions of early industrialisation in which it arose. By reverting to the bureaucratic methods of Tsarism and the enforced rigours of rural depopulation and factory discipline, was it not betraying the ideology of the left? This seems a much more important criticism than the debate about the defects of Stalin's personality which Khruschev introduced apparently as an alibi for what the party had done and intended to continue doing. It is quite true that, of all the Russians who suffered under Stalinism, the party members suffered most both proportionally in numbers and personally in the mental and physical tortures of the series of purges launched in 1934. The party ruled, however, both over the consciences of its members and over the lives of the Russian people at large. The party must be judged for what happened in Russia and must face Deutscher's charge of 'the unfinished revolution' (**36**). The ideological left in power achieved much, but much less than it had promised. It provided Europe, the world and, ironically, the right with the model of totalitarian dictatorship (**44**). In doing so, it remained the loyal heir of Lenin.

A discussion of the successes and failures of the Social Democratic governments of the moderate left in the interwar period may seem in a sense irrelevant in a book which has defined its terms of reference as the study of political extremism. These governments deserve attention, however, for several reasons. They presented a new phenomenon in European politics, for not even the moderate left had formed a government in the nineteenth century. Their failures contribute to the explanation of why parliamentary democracy went into eclipse. They also demonstrate the effect on Europe of the Bolshevik revolution. Everywhere that they achieved power or a share in it, these parties faced a cruel dilemma. If they adopted radically leftist policies, they inflamed the reaction from the right. If they practised restraint they incurred the scorn and hatred of the radical left as 'social Fascists'. Their dilemma was that of the twentieth-century centre. In attempting to defend as well as to advance, to change and at the same time to preserve, they demonstrated both the virtues and the defects of parliamentary democracy in critical times. They deserve perhaps a great deal of admiration for certain qualities of restraint and stoical courage. It is also possible to see why they became an object of despair to some radicals and of contempt to others.

Once again Germany provides the clearest example of a trend (**35**). The Social Democrats, as the largest single party within the Reichstag, took over power on the eve of the armistice of 1918 as the residual legatees of the imperial Reich. Their first decisions disclosed the nature of the problem which was to face them. By accepting the continuation of parliamentary government, they precipitated the formation of the German Communist party and made themselves an enemy on the left. By accepting the terms of Versailles, however inevitable such a decision might have been, they incurred the displeasure of the nationalist right. The armed forces, traditionally the grey eminence of German politics, supported them because the alternative at that moment seemed Communist revolution. In return the Socialists had for the next ten years to allow the army, officially reduced almost to nothing by the treaty, to maintain its independent political existence until its leaders decided that the republic might be dispensed with in favour of Hitler. Meanwhile the Socialists refrained from radical policies, allowing inflation to climb rather than risking a tax programme which might further alienate the right.

The Socialists' difficulties were clearly not entirely of their own making and none of the other parties of the centre showed greater dynamism or enjoyed greater success in a series of centre–left coalitions. Socialism was resolutely non-radical. Its internal development, in the words of one historian, displayed three dominant characteristics: 'bossification, ossification and bourgeoisification' (**35**). If it became no more than an electoral machine or the 'passive instrument of trade unionism', then these unheroic virtues played their part in maintaining the republic during these years, notably when solid strike action defeated the Kapp Putsch and helped to isolate Hitler's Munich demonstration. In 1929, however, the Socialists took a fatal step towards the destruction of the republic when they withdrew from the coalition government rather than support a reduction in welfare benefits as an antidote to the economic crisis. This breakdown led to the period of emergency, presidential government from which Hitler emerged as chancellor. In 1932 the Socialist state government of Prussia, although it could have tried to rally support and call on the militant organisation of the *Reichsbanner*, accepted its dismissal by von Papen under threat of force and relied on the coming elections to restore it to power. In 1933 the Socialists still received seven million votes and with a considerable degree of stolid heroism resisted all the overt pressures which persuaded other parties to vote for the Enabling Act and the establishment of Nazi tyranny. Their members were then dispersed into exile or concentration camps.

What else could German Socialism have done? Statistics have already been quoted to show that its electoral support was constant but insufficient to defeat Nazism by democratic means. Allen shows that any attempts at *Reichsbanner* militancy in Thalburg served only to confirm the popular confusion of Socialism with Communism and strengthen the stampede to the right. That the Communists contributed so powerfully, both positively and negatively, to Socialism's failure in Germany is an ironic illustration of the forces which were at work destroying European democracy.

Next door in Austria, as has already been noted, similar forces were in play (**47, 68**). Social Democrats briefly formed the first postwar and postrevolutionary government. They lasted long enough to experience the same amputation and subsequent sniping of the Communist left and to incur the same right-wing indignation at their acceptance of the humiliating terms of the treaty of Saint-Germain. In Vienna, however, they enjoyed a stronger position, similar to that of the socialists in Berlin, and disposed of both the armed forces and the paramilitary *Schutzbund*. Viennese Socialism was confidently radical. Banks and businesses were taxed, along with private property-owners, to finance an educational and housing programme whose proudest monuments were the Karl Marx and Goethe Houses.

In the truncated and largely rural Austria of Saint-Germain Vienna and a few other towns were red islands in a black sea of Catholic conservatism. The Christian Socialists represented a wider following and the *Heimwehr* recruited in the provinces, promising to 'clean up' Vienna by a process which had nothing to do with slum clearance. From 1929 until 1934 this situation escalated to the tragic conflict which was described at the beginning of this book. The economic crisis of Europe, the most critical phase of which began with

51

the failure of the Vienna bank *Creditanstalt*, led to government policies which threatened the livelihood and welfare of the working class. The rising success of Nazism across the border brought an air of competition to the extremism of the right. The Christian Socialist Dollfuss perhaps aimed to appear as a moderate in the sharpening conflict when he appealed for national unity. His measures, however, appeared as an attack on the strongholds of the left. Beginning with an order to the army to occupy the railway stations and break a strike precipitated by wage and pension cuts among railwaymen, he went on to suspend the parliamentary constitution, to propose government control of the trade unions and to abolish the autonomy of Vienna. The *Heimwehr* took these policies as an encouragement to strike at Socialism, first in Linz. The Vienna Socialists, having pinned all their hopes on their constitutional position which had now been destroyed, called a general strike. The sequel has already been described. The left in power had again proved inadequate to resist the right.

The fate of the British Labour Party in these years was less dramatic but equally ignominious. Two spells of governmental power, each time under the frustrations of a Liberal coalition, ended precipitately. On the first occasion, in 1924, accusations of being soft on Communism caused first its resignation and then its electoral defeat. On the second, demands similar to those made of the German Socialists for a reduction in unemployment benefits resulted in a split in the cabinet and the party and the decision of the leaders to join a national coalition with the Conservatives. Philip Snowden, more orthodox than the orthodox in his fiscal policies and Ramsay MacDonald, more bourgeois than the bourgeoisie in his desire for an end to party conflict and almost aristocratic in his social ambitions, have borne the brunt of left wing criticism for these capitulations. In their defence the same question may be asked—what else could they have done? They tried to make Socialism respectable and introduced a housing policy which was to last. To have made the official left in Britain more militant might in the long run have delayed still further its emergence as the second major party. In the short run it might have stirred to greater violence the tendencies to political extremism which had already distinguished themselves on both sides during the General Strike of 1926. By its moderation the Labour Party helped to reinforce democracy in Britain.

The left in France followed an idiosyncratic course which, though it brought it nearer to extremism than ever happened in Britain, yet maintained the stability both of the Socialist movement and of the parliamentary republic. At the Congress of Tours in 1920 it split over the question of adherence to Comintern, and the Communist party was founded. Next year the Communists split the unity of the trade union movement in a similar way. The special nature of the French Communist movement has already been mentioned. The parliamentary Socialists displayed the same predominance of age over youth and caution over radicalism. Radicalism was the title of the French political centre, but for the historian it could be as misleading a description as the *Cartel des Gauches* which formed a coalition government in 1924. This was a Radical-Socialist group which toyed with the idea of a capital levy but achieved nothing except a flight of capital and the restoration of the bourgeois *Bloc National*. French Conservatives were equally cautious in a situation where coalition cabinets were difficult to sustain and where civil conflict remained always a possibility.

In the thirties right-wing extremism came to the streets of Paris in circumstances which have already been described. Whether the *Camelots du Roi, Jeunesses Patriotes* and *Croix de Feu*, as divided as the left among themselves, contemplated power has been debated by historians. Gallic caution, as important a national characteristic as alleged volatility, reasserted itself on the left in face of the potential challenge. In the elections of 1936 a *rassemblement populaire* emerged to form a government, led by the socialist Blum, supported by Radicals and also by the Communists, admittedly in response to the new Stalinist party line. It was a negative rather than a positive left alliance but it reflected a determined working class will, shown in the growth of trade union membership at the time, and it registered positive achievements in the labour field. The Matignon agreements secured employers' recognition of collective negotiation, an immediate wage increase of seven to fifteen per cent, and a forty-hour week. Except for the last, these reforms remained when the Popular Front had gone. As on previous and later occasions, the French labour movement had shown what it could achieve when it achieved unity first (7).

The Fascist leagues were also outlawed. From then on, however, the achievements of the Popular Front ended. A new flight of capital and of gold ensued and the Senate would not empower Blum to prevent it. He was caught between radical action and the threat of renewed political activity on the right. More to the point, perhaps, he was caught in a situation which has regularly debilitated the left in power in a capitalist society: a lack of confidence shown by the world of finance. Like some other Socialist moderates before and since he 'paused' in his programme of social reform and devalued the franc. Foreign policy had caught him in a similar dilemma. His left supporters urged him to intervene on the side of the Socialist Republic in the Spanish civil war. The centre would not tolerate it and the National government of Britain, or so Blum feared, would have broken its links with him and left France isolated in Fascist Europe except for a Soviet alliance which he suspected as deeply as he did the motives of his Communist allies. Blum resigned. The Popular Front had not been without its successes. Indeed it may have saved France from civil war. It had faced all the problems of the moderate left in power, however, and had been overcome by them. From now on the French right and perhaps some British conservatives muttered 'Better Hitler than Blum'. The Communists, in 1939, set off on the new tack of 'revolutionary defeatism' which followed the Hitler–Stalin pact. These developments help to explain why France fell in 1940.

At the risk of multiplying examples to the point of confusing the reader, one more left régime must briefly be described to complete the picture. It is the one example of Anarchism in power which Europe provides, apart from the brief régime of Nestor Makhno in the Ukraine during the Russian revolution.

A simple explanation of why the Anarchist tradition took root in Spain is hard to come by. James Joll (**42**) lists some of the suggested possibilities. Earlier in this book, the reader's attention has been drawn to the particularly backward state of Spain in the early twentieth century, a condition shared with parts of Italy and Russia. Peasant poverty was total under a system of archaic feudalism. Sections of the working class, for instance miners, were peasants at one remove and encountered the process of industrialisation under its most primitive organisational forms. Such circumstances may be thought likely to produce a form of social protest less sophisticated than either the parliamentary Socialism of more advanced states or even Communism. Spanish Anarchism was also ferociously anti-clerical in a country where the Church continued to hold enormous secular wealth and power. There was also the separatist regionalism of Catalonia and Andalusia, suspicious and resentful of government from Madrid. Whatever the full explanation, Anarchist economic and political action began in the nineteenth century in Spain and flashed out, fiercely and briefly, in Barcelona during the *semana tragica* of 1909.

It reappeared in the Spanish civil war. On this occasion the rising of the left was a reaction to the activity of the right. General Franco's revolt against the Radical-Socialist coalition of the Republic stimulated the Barcelona Anarchists to their own revolution. It lived up to Sorel's demands for violence [**doc. 3**]. Churches were burned, prisons opened, an estimated 500 people killed and 3000 wounded. Middle class people removed their hats and ties in order to appear as proletarians. The Anarchist régime which ensued is famous from the pages of George Orwell's *Homage to Catalonia* (**20**) [**doc. 13**]. The workers took over the factories and organised small tradesmen into syndicates. Outside the city attempts to establish collective farms met with peasant resistance comparable to that which Communism had encountered in Russia, but within Barcelona society was Communism plus.

Perhaps for this reason the Spanish Communist party distrusted and disliked the Anarchists. Under Moscow's direction they had joined the Popular Front to defend the Republic against the Nationalist right, but they aimed to impose their own discipline within that Front. The aid which Moscow alone among European governments gave to the republic was a powerful factor in strengthening their claims. The Anarchists were not susceptible to discipline. When Durruti's column, a famous libertarian fighting force, was summoned to the defence of Madrid, it refused to take orders from the government. Indeed it refused to go into action at all when first confronted by Franco's guns. Under the pressure of the war and the Nationalist advance Anarchists reluctantly accepted ministerial posts, but the alliance of the moderate, Communist and libertarian left did not last long. The responsibility for the outbreak of fighting in Barcelona on 3 May 1937 is as obscure and debated as that for Durruti's death in action at the front, which may have been at the hand of political opponents on the government side. Franco's agents may have been active in Barcelona, stirring up the already simmering conflict between the Republic and the Communists, on the one side, and the Anarchists and Trotskyist POUM on the other. In a week of fighting the Anarchists were defeated; 400 people were killed and 1000 wounded. The power of the Communists within the

E                                                                                           55

Republican government increased and they demanded the suppression of the dissident left. Thus Anarchism in power, an expression which is itself almost a contradiction in terms, fell. The circumstances resembled those of Socialism's defeat in Vienna. On this occasion, however, the executioners were members of the left themselves (**42, 65**).

This is a theme which has now been shown to run through the whole story of the left in power. Socialists in power were attempting to establish for the first time in European history governments which reflected the will and the needs of the working class and of the ideological left. This task alone was enormous, since their inexperience was confronted by the expert hostility of social groups who had wielded economic and political power for a century or more. To this problem the Communists added the weakening effect of an internecine struggle on the left. They destroyed Anarchism and undermined the authority of the moderate labour movement. On the occasions when they supported it their support served chiefly to alienate the right still further.

On the other hand, the Communists built a state in Russia, while Socialism failed to build a government elsewhere. Their success there was the basis of their claim to lead the left. Their methods there were, in their final form, an uncompromising totalitarianism. This form of government became a model for dictatorships and was paralleled and imitated by the right in power (**35**).

# 7 The Right in Power

As the period between the two world wars has receded into history, historians have tended to emphasise that neither Italian Fascism nor even German Nazism practised a totalitarianism as rigidly comprehensive as that of Communist Russia (58). This is clearly a question of the difference between perspective and experience. To a mass of ordinary citizens who lived through any of these régimes, and particularly to critics and victims of the ruling parties, the negation of freedom and the omnipresence of the police and the party, not to mention the atrocities carried out in the name of ideology and in the interests of the rulers, must have presented a single and depressing picture. To the historians certain differences will be apparent. Russian Communism ruled a country vast and backward and employed the traditional methods of the Tsarist bureaucracy to which a largely illiterate people had become passively accustomed. Italy was a more diverse and volatile society, even if the roots of parliamentary government went little deeper than in eastern Europe in time. Germany was an advanced society in which a multitude of vocal social pressure groups could not be silenced and ignored in their entirety by a régime which had come to power on a popular mandate and which aimed to stay there.

Mussolini lacked even a political strategy such as that which Lenin devised under the slogan of the dictatorship of the proletariat. There was no consistent plan behind his erratic course to power and not even a party discipline (**7, 46, 49**) [**doc. 6**]. His first notion, after the battle with the red communes had made Fascism a popular political party with votes and parliamentary seats, seems to have been to form a coalition with the moderate Socialist and Catholic parties. The local *squadristi* and their backers required him to turn to the nationalist bloc however. Again after the march on Rome a similar indecision appears. Making an impromptu speech on the first anniversary of the occasion, Mussolini referred to a period of five years as the probable duration of his régime. Then, pausing, he corrected the figure to sixty (**46**).

## The Practice

In 1924 the Nationalist bloc won two-thirds of the parliamentary seats, in an election carried out with the active interference of the Fascist militia whose actions were ignored by the police. When parliament assembled the Socialist deputy Matteotti protested courageously and vehemently against the methods employed. Within a few days he had disappeared, almost certainly murdered by the Fascists, and a Roman crowd demonstrated angrily beneath Mussolini's windows. The prime minister seemed shaken, promised a broader-based cabinet and a ban on illegal political methods. At this point the provincial Fascist leaders forced his hand with a threat of renewed political violence unless he maintained the party's grip on power. Mussolini now accepted public responsibility for the violence which had already occurred and claimed that force was and remained an essential of Fascism. The government was purged of moderates, the extremist Roberto Farinacci became general secretary of a national Fascist party and the development of a non-parliamentary, totalitarian régime proceeded without further interruption.

Mussolini never attempted a purge of his party similar to those with which both Hitler and Stalin consolidated their leadership. He also left real power in the hands of the King from whom he received his first appointment. In 1943 it was a vote of no confidence in the Fascist Grand Council which authorised the King to remove him, though neither Fascism nor the monarchy survived his fall by many months. Mussolini seems never to have been the master of Fascism: but Fascism was nothing without his charismatic leadership.

In its government of Italy Fascism was never absolute. Apart from the residual authority of the monarchy, it came to terms with the Pope which recognised his independence, and left capitalism untouched in its operations. The chief characteristic of the corporate state, as has been mentioned, was the suppression of the rights of labour. In this, as in its anti-parliamentarism, Fascism was a totalitarianism of the right. Its negative achievements were its successes. Almost everything else was propaganda. The trains ran on time. A practical effect of the corporate organisation of the economy was to depress wages and thus encourage industrial development. By 1939 Italy was able to feed herself in grain, but her balance of payments remained constantly adverse, and little was done to correct the historic imbalance between north and south. Whether the Mafia was suppressed is dubious. Fascist foreign policy may also be described as negative rather than positive in its effects. 'War alone,' said the propagandist Mussolini, 'brings up to their highest tension all human energies and puts the stamp of nobility upon the peoples who have the courage to meet it' [**doc. 6**]: but war for Italy meant the worthless conquests of Abyssinia and Albania and a servile dependence upon Hitler which ended in the fall of Fascism (**52**).

Hitler, like Lenin, developed a theory of power while still powerless. It is set out in *Mein Kampf* and skilfully combines the drive to totalitarianism with the compromises required to gain power within a developed and democratically constituted state:

> Popular support is the first element which is necessary for the creation of authority. But an authority resting on that foundation alone is still quite frail, uncertain and vacillating. Hence everyone who finds himself vested with an authority that is based only on popular support must take measures to improve and consolidate the foundations of that authority by the creation of force. Accordingly, we must look upon power, that is to say the capacity to use force, as the second foundation on which all authority is based. This foundation is more stable and secure, but not always stronger, than the first. If popular support and power are united together and can endure for a certain time, then an authority may arise which is based on a still stronger foundation, that of tradition. And, finally, if popular support, power and tradition are united together, then the authority based on them may be looked upon as invincible (**18**).

How much popularity Hitler enjoyed and how skilfully he obtained it has been explained in an earlier chapter. The element of forceful power was added by the process of *Gleichschaltung* which Bullock has called 'the revolution from above' (**54**) and which began with the totalitarian powers granted by the last Reichstag in the Enabling Bill of 1933. From then on Hitler ruled by decree and by force. Reich governors took over the functions of state governments and the Labour Front superseded both employers' organisations and trades unions. Universities and the civil service were purged of critics of the régime and a 'German Church' was created to subordinate religion to the superior ideology of the state. Above all the police and the party ruled. The Gestapo played the role of the Cheka and its successors, the OGPU, NKUD and KGB in Russia, and the party organisation was represented at provincial, city and district level and even within each block of flats. The penalties for dissension, imposed by the People's Courts, led to the concentration camp. In a more positive way the drives for popularity plus control were combined in the various youth movements and in *Strength through Joy*, a cultural and leisure organisation which subordinated to the party and to ideology every pastime, in Carsten's phrase, from bowling clubs to bee-keeping (**46**).

It may be objected that the Third Reich did not last long enough to implement Hitler's third 'foundation of authority'—the authority of tradition. Everything that the Nazi régime did, however, was designed to invest it with the mantle of Imperial Germany. The whole appeal of the movement looked backwards to the rural and military past and forwards to a continued territorial expansion which had been the policy of Frederick the Great, Bismarck and their successors up to and during the first world war, and which Hitler described as the rightful destiny of the Aryan race in its search for living space. This, along with the redemption of the shame of Versailles and the unification of all German-speaking peoples, was the basis of his foreign policy. In more concrete terms, he sealed an alliance with tradition by the circumstances in which he came to power. The coalition with the aristocratic Nationalist party, the ceremony of installation in the Imperial chapel at Potsdam, attended by Hindenburg and the Crown Prince, the final accession of the army's support by the Blomberg pact, all these steps linked Hitler's régime with a tradition which he had no need to create.

These alliances meant compromises on Hitler's part, of course. The price of the right's support was the liquidation of the gangsters of the SA and the Socialist doctrinaires within the Nazi movement. The price of industry's support was to leave industry untrammelled. The civil service was required to administer a sophisticated state quite different from that which Russian Communism inherited. The voters must be satisfied even if elections were no more and even the working class must be harnessed to the régime. From the continuing existence of these varied pressure groups, historians have created a picture of the Third Reich as a jungle of competing interests and inconsistent policies over which Hitler ruled with no less but no more power than an oriental despot in his palace. Thus the German economy is seen to have recovered from the depression more by its own buoyancy than as the result of processes which distorted its structure and balance. Full employment was a political goal in conflict with economic recovery, obtained by the creation of jobs, the overmanning of shrinking industries and a minimal direction of labour until the shortage of labour in key industries such as construction, metal and mining was acute. It also brought continued inflation as consumer living standards and wages were allowed to rise unchecked. Government spending rose because of public works schemes and also because the régime had promised to assist small farmers and guarantee their holdings and their prices, whereas the economic demand of an industrial society was for larger units and market prices.

Above all government spending was directed towards rearmament. Whether this was the deliberate goal of Nazism is still a matter of considerable dispute among historians. It may have been rather a response to the pressure of the military–industrial complex which Goering represented and whose policies Dr Schacht, the first economics minister of the Reich, opposed in favour of retrenchment and national self-sufficiency. On trial at Nuremberg, Schacht repeatedly maintained that he had tried to save Germany from a war policy. The prestige and profits involved were too great. The level of military demand was such that risk was almost eliminated for entrepreneurs in the capital goods industries. Some steel manufacturers havered at the possibility of overproduction but Goering's threat of nationalisation brought them to heel. The only remaining opposition came from the Labour Front, which resented the necessary rundown of other industries and the redirection of labour.

By 1938, therefore, the German economy was strained to breaking point by this multiplicity of conflicting aims. It is possible that Hitler's war policy resulted as much from this intolerable situation, which only war, territorial expansion and annexed raw materials could resolve, as from any other political or ideological considerations. It would be reckless to rule these out, as it would be to conclude that because in five years Nazi rule had failed to become completely totalitarian or to effect the social revolution that it had promised, it would never have done so. As with Communist Russia, the situation when the Third Reich fell was that of a revolution which might have been unfinished. As with Russia, it is also possible to conclude that the revolution was never intended to take place.

A further parallel between Nazi Germany and Soviet Russia is furnished by considering the career of the *Schutz Staffeln*. This organisation, formed under Heinrich Himmler, and attached to

61

Hitler's service by a special oath of loyalty, replaced the SA after carrying out its liquidation in 1934. In the prewar years its best-known activities were those of the Gestapo, but during the war its responsibilities were enormously increased. In David Schoenbaum's summary:

It administered occupied territories as a kind of self-contained Ministry of the Interior and maintained itself economically with autonomous enterprises. Unlike other Nazi institutions, which aspired to one or other of the State functions, the SS potentially superseded the State, reproducing it within its own ranks and even endowing it with administrative novelties hitherto unknown in more conventional practice. An interesting example was the policy of holding ranks in the so-called Security Service, the nucleus of the political police, artificially low so that rank and authority no longer coincided. It was thus not only theoretically but practically possible that an officer of the Security Service could be superior to an SS officer who outranked (**58**).

A comparison with the function and workings of the Communist party in the Soviet Union is irresistible. The political commissar, the state within the state, the power and responsibilities undefined by law or even administrative routine all link the two organisations. The SS in Germany represented the career open to the talents. It was also the special repository of Nazi ideology. Its members were an élite, indoctrinated with Aryanism. Plans were laid for the formation of a specially pure, Aryan, SS state in Burgundy after the war. The war gave the SS its special status, just as the civil war made the Communist party supreme in Russia. Would the SS have gone on to radicalise German society and fulfil Hitler's ideological dreams? Would it have become, like the Soviet Communist party in its mature years, no more than a privileged and oppressive bureaucracy, itself requiring to be purged or revitalised? The question is imponderable because the war destroyed the SS. The best-known of its low-ranking but high-powered officers has become Adolf Eichmann, and the best-known of its functions the 'final solution of the Jewish question' in which he participated. In historical terms the SS must be judged by what it did (**59**).

This must also be true of Nazism as a whole. Its signal achievements were, in the practical field, to precipitate and lose a war; in the ideological field, to persecute the Jews. They were negative achievements which served only to distort and to retard the twentieth-century development of Germany. They may therefore be compared with those of Fascism in Italy, in Spain and elsewhere. The Nationalist alliance in Spain incorporated the ideological Falangist party, with its syndicalist programme for the Spanish economy, but the founder of the Falange, José Antonio, died in prison and was most useful as a propagandist martyr (**7, 66**). The corporate state did not revitalise the Spanish economy, which remained a system of small-scale industries and immense rural estates. Only American capital has injected new blood into this system.

The same picture of economic and social immobility emerges from a consideration of the central European régimes. The corporate state which Dollfuss's Fatherland Front established in Austria was 'for industrialists . . . a façade behind which most of the capitalistic practices that the corporative system aimed at abolishing could go on unhindered. The radical social and economic reforms envisaged by sincere believers in the new system were never carried out' (**47**). Dollfuss was as consistently anti-Nazi as he was anti-Socialist, but his assassination prefaced the union of Austria and Germany and the Austrian right thereupon 'ceased to exist as a political movement'. In Hungary a series of would-be charismatic leaders faltered before the stony conservatism of Horthy and the only legislative achievement was a series of anti-Jewish laws similar to those which in Germany deprived them of basic social rights. Horthy resisted the policy of 'the final solution,' however, until 1944, by which time he was completely disillusioned with the Nazis whose occupation had forced Hungary into the war on the Axis powers' side. His proposal to surrender to the Russians led to his deposition by the proto-Nazi Arrow Cross, which lasted long enough to sacrifice 50,000 more Jews to Eichmann before it fled before the Red Army's advance (**47**).

Fascist leaders with radical ideas flashed through the history of eastern European states. Weber has drawn attention to the idealism as well as the crude anti-semitism of the Rumanian Codreanu; but Codreanu died in a government prison and his Legion was suppressed as a subversive threat by the conservative General Antonescu who then submitted to Hitler. Quasi-monarchical dictatorships in Bulgaria, Yugoslavia and Greece proved powerless either to bring economic development or to save the monarchs from German deposition. By the end of the second world war, Communism was bidding for power, more or less successfully, in all these countries.

63

### The Practice

Thus the record of the right in power amounts to as little as that of the left in the period between the wars. Its radicalism, such as it was, amounted to nothing in practice. Perhaps it may be regarded as more successful because it achieved the negative ends which had been probably the most important and certainly the most popular features of its ideological programme. It had suppressed the left and persecuted the Jews. Ironically, the first of these achievements proved quite impermanent. While democratic societies survived Fascism and Communism as well, the régimes of the right, except in Spain and Portugal, went down in the war into which Hitler had drawn them. Upon their ruins Communism celebrated its grim victories.

# 8 Left and Right in Conflict

The antagonism of Socialism and Anti-Socialism has been the continuing theme of this essay. For a generation of those who saw politics in ideological terms, however, this conflict reached its climax in the Spanish civil war. Some regarded the Spanish war as a test of democracy's ability to survive. Others concluded that democracy in Spain, as elsewhere, had already failed and that the contest was to decide whether Socialism or Fascism should be the wave of the future. The Spanish issues seemed starkly defined, removing any necessity for mental reservation or qualified support. On the left stood the popular front—Radicals, Socialists, Communists, Trotskyists and even Anarchists for once combined in a common cause. On the right appeared a classically reactionary alliance of monarchists and clericals, landowners and capitalists, army officers and ideological Fascists. The clarity of definition and the simplicity of the issues at stake seem to take the historian back to the earlier period of European history when the concepts of left and right first appeared.

The established Communist and Fascist powers assiduously fed this situation with the propaganda of dialectical conflict. The parliamentary states showed a characteristic combination of caution, timidity and indifference. Stalin had by now embarked on a policy of building bridges with western Europe for purposes both of commerce and defence. Defined in the language of Comintern the policy was a united front against Fascism. It was also perhaps desirable to distract the attention of the international left from the saturnine holocaust of the purges which were decimating the Russian party membership. Some of the men whom Stalin feared were sent to Spain.

The effective contribution of Russian aid to the republican front is another matter and one on which historians' opinions differ. The positive assistance of Russian tanks and the Communist-led International Brigades to the defence of Madrid was probably decisive (**20, 65**). In practical terms the republic paid for every tank and gun by transferring its gold reserves to Russia. In political terms the price of Communist intervention was Communist ascendancy. The effects of this on the unity of the left and its morale have already been described.

Once again also the Communist support had the fatal effect of feeding the propaganda of the right. The motives of Germany in sending the Condor Legion of bombers to Nationalist Spain were partly, like those of Russia, a military exercise. The German High Command saw an opportunity to test the tactics of *Blitzkrieg* attack in laboratory conditions. In military terms the experiment was an unqualified success. Mussolini also hoped for a propaganda success and gave valuable assistance to the Nationalists by interdicting Republican shipping. In propagandist terms, Fascism and Nazism gained more from their intervention in Spain than cheap military glory. The signature of the Anti-Comintern Pact of November 1937 brought the ideological conflict to an international level. Hitler and Mussolini, whose individual attempts at national aggrandisement in Austria, in Abyssinia and in the Rhineland had in the previous two years provoked the hostility of Britain and France, still the major powers in Europe, now acquired a new respectability as the champions of international anti-Communism. From now on the dictators gained advocates at the highest political levels in France and Britain and in 1938 at Munich a determined attempt was made to bring Germany and Italy back into the concert of Europe.

All this was done at the expense of the Spanish republic, for Britain and France now agreed on the policy of non-intervention. The new alignment also brought to an end any determined attempts to forge a lasting defence pact between western Europe and the Soviet Union. Thus the diplomatic victor of the Spanish Civil War was Hitler, whose hands were now freed to pursue Germany's European ambitions.

Those ambitions had always included expansion to the east at the expense of Russia. In *Mein Kampf*, Hitler demanded that 'the German people must be assured the territorial area which is necessary for it to exist on this earth'. In such an eastern policy, ideology and economic necessity combined. Russia occupied territory, in the Ukraine, which Germany coveted. Russia was also the home of the international Judaeo-Bolshevik conspiracy. Once again the ideological issue was clear and appreciated as such by the international supporters of Communist Russia as well as by the German population at large. The impact on the true believer's mind of the Nazi-Soviet non-aggression pact of 1939 was therefore numbing. Hitler himself commented that 'We had the task of converting to a completely reverse opinion those whom we had originally made into fanatical opponents of Russia. Fortunately the spirit of party solidarity held firm' (**6**). The effect on the mind of international Communism has been recorded by Claud Cockburn, then a correspondent of the *Daily Worker* and of *Pravda*:

> No one old enough to have been politically conscious at that time is likely to forget the bubble of passions, the frantic accusations and counter-accusations, the 'agonizing re-appraisals', the re-affirmations of faith, the hubbub of emotions, which thereupon broke out. And, of course, people too young to have been there must by now find a lot of the excitement irrelevant and incomprehensible. It was real enough that night.

The reader of this book, it is hoped, will not find such emotions incomprehensible. An alliance of Communism and Nazism, left and right, was a complete and cynical reversal of the ideological politics of the preceding twenty years. It can be explained in terms of the military interests of both sides. Hitler, like every German strategist since Germany became a state, was anxious to avoid the situation of a two-front war on east and west. Stalin, having thrown the defence of Russia into chaos by his purge of the high command, was also playing for time. The Nazi-Soviet pact was not the final chapter in Nazi-Soviet relations or in the struggle between left and right. Within a short space of time the German *panzer* divisions had invaded Russia and Evelyn Waugh's fictional Catholic hero, Guy Crouchback, was gazing with incredulous disgust at the sword of Stalingrad displayed in a place of honour in Westminster Abbey. By 1945 the Red Army was playing a far more effective role in the extension of Communist power in eastern and central Europe than Comintern, which was wound up in 1943, had ever done. In these areas the left won the final victory in its struggle with the right and the scale and nature of the ideological struggle became that of the Cold War to which every reader will be accustomed.

The Nazi–Soviet pact therefore did not mark the end of the conflict of the interwar period, or of political ideology. It may, however, serve to raise some concluding questions in the reader's mind. These may relate to the authenticity of ideology itself. How genuine was the belief of the ideologues in their own slogans, so few of which they ever put into practice and whose principles proved so flexible when measured against the exigencies of power? The effect of ideological propaganda, on the other hand, cannot be held in doubt. Millions fought, suffered and died as its willing or unwilling sacrificial victims. Were they the victims of their own or others' delusions, or even of the manipulations of their hopes and fears by men whose only aim was power?

# Part Three

# ASSESSMENT

# 9 Conclusion

An essay which begins, as this one does, with the study of ideas and moves on to the realities of political power and the apparent duplicities of great power diplomacy, is bound to raise questions such as those with which the previous chapter concluded. In the case of Fascism, Nazism and Communism, such a process of study draws attention increasingly to the similarities between the totalitarian régimes. The differences which remain can largely be explained in terms of the different social structures and national traditions of the states in which the régimes operated. Thus Nazism or Spanish Fascism, for instance, come to be seen as phases in the national history of Germany and Spain whose characteristics are those of national history as a whole. European Communism, even at its fullest extent after the second world war, seems less an ideological movement, or even an international conspiracy, than an extension of Soviet foreign policy.

Clearly there is a great deal of substance in this view, a substance whose weight is increased by the fact that historians who hold it tend to be those with direct experience of one or other of the régimes in question or even of more than one (**1, 6**). It is the inhumanity and cynicism of totalitarian government which distinguishes all the governments of Communism and Fascism alike, in their experience, rather than ideological distinctions.

Important a qualification as it is, however, this point of view seems an unnecessarily narrow and distorted definition of the extremist movements. It tends to ignore very real differences of social and economic policy and also the factors which were common to eastern and western, developed and underdeveloped Europe. In its understandable reaction against the tyranny of ideology, it tends to dismiss the importance of ideology both in enlisting members for the activist movements and in winning massive popular support. Unless the historian gives his attention to such considerations, most of the history of this period and these movements becomes inexplicable.

### Assessment

What gives ideological politics their attraction? Seymour Lipset argues (5) that parliamentary democracy is a highly sophisticated method of politics. Its conventions of tolerance for opposition, reasoned argument and gradual change call for an intelligence, self-confidence and restraint among both politicians and voters which the masses and their leaders often lack. Lipset describes these characteristics as sophistication and ego security. Where they are absent, a more impatient, intolerant and fundamentally more un-intelligent view of politics arises. Issues are seen in black and white, preferably in personalised, 'demonological' terms. Action, prompt and sweeping, is called for and promised.

Political attitudes which spring from such psychological roots are not necessarily to be deplored. Hugh Thomas notes that many of the British volunteers to the International Brigades 'appear to have been persons who derived some outlet through which to purge some private grief or maladjustment' (65). In moral terms, however, as Thomas insists, they were idealists. Tolerance and restraint can be admirable qualities, but they can also be described as a complacent apathy towards social anachronisms and injustices. Society needs radicals and, if the majority of people require to have a situation presented to them in simple terms before they can appreciate the need to change it, then the radical can perform a service by drawing this picture.

Nevertheless, it is a dangerous step to take reason out of politics. Mussolini, Hitler and Stalin were unsophisticated men with notably insecure egos and their idealism can only be called perverted at its best. The mass radicalism which such leaders aroused, particularly perhaps on the right, was directed less at renewing society than at dragging it back into a primitive past. The instincts to which it appealed, and this is true of left as well as right, were more often envy or hatred than more positive emotions. They divided Europe and European society rather than united it and retarded or even destroyed its development rather than contributing to growth.

It is important to note that such instincts were common to every class of society and that the precondition of their being aroused lay in economic and social catastrophe. The first world war, the succeed-ing economic crises and the Bolshevik revolution itself were the events which destroyed the 'ego security' of lords and peasants, capi-tal and labour and also, and perhaps most significantly, the middle classes on whose demands for stability and moderation the system of parliamentary democracy had been built. When they too deserted it, its days were numbered and the field was clear for the ideologists of the left and right.

Two democracies—Britain and France—and substantial groups within other societies resisted the seductions of extremism. This also is important to note. It emphasises that well-rooted loyalties can be difficult to break and that democracy is not inevitably doomed in the twentieth century. Since the rise of extremism was the product of nationalist politics and the process of industrialisation, however, it could recur so long as these historical conditions exist. Indeed it has recurred under such conditions in Asia, in Africa and in Latin America since 1945, and the conflict of left and right has moved beyond Europe to a world arena.

In doing so, it has extended and modified the definitions of left and right just as the advent of Marxism, Fascism and Nazism did in their time. As Russian Communism and its satellite extensions have maintained an unrelenting totalitarianism, unaccompanied by any noticeable advance towards the classless society, the dynamic of the left has been transferred to the peasant socialism which Mao Tse Tung represents at its most successful. Vietnam has become, in the 1960s, the *cause célèbre* of the left that Spain was in the 1930s. In western Europe Anarchism has sprung to life again, particularly among students whose sophistication is not accompanied by a marked degree of ego security (**45**).

A dynamic left has produced the historic reaction on the right. Fascism and Nazism died, discredited, with the second world war. Anti-Communist, non-parliamentary governments have come into existence in Greece, in Asia, in Africa and in Latin America. A simplified, demonological view of politics characterises the cold war across the world, in democratic as in Communist countries. Most significantly, perhaps, for the future, the language of left and right has entered into the relations of the white and coloured races. Afro-Asian radicals, wherever they are found, discuss politics and society in Marxist terms. Anti-coloured emotions, at their least sophisticated, are couched in terms which derive from the conceptions of Nazi and Fascist racism.

Thus prejudice and idealism, ideology and extremism, are not dead. The record of what happened to Europe in the first half of the twentieth century may contain perhaps some indications of what is likely to become of civilised society when such passions are unleashed.

# Part Four

# DOCUMENTS

CLASSICAL MARXISM: THE COMMUNIST MANIFESTO

The history of all hitherto existing society is the history of class struggles. . . .

The modern bourgeois society that has sprouted from the ruins of feudal society, has not done away with class antagonisms. It has but established new classes, new conditions of oppression, new forms of struggle in place of the old ones.

Our epoch, the epoch of the bourgeoisie, possesses, however, this distinctive feature: it has simplified the class antagonisms. Society as a whole is more and more splitting up into two great hostile camps, into two great classes directly facing each other—bourgeoisie and proletariat. . . .

Modern industry has converted the little workshop of the patriarchal master into the great factory of the industrial capitalist. Masses of labourers, crowded into the factory, are organised like soldiers. As privates of the industrial army, they are placed under the command of a positive hierarchy of officers and sergeants. Not only are they slaves of the bourgeois class, and of the bourgeois state; they are daily and hourly enslaved by the machine, by the overseer, and, above all, by the individual bourgeois manufacturer himself. The more openly this despotism proclaims gain to be its end and aim, the more petty, the more hateful and the more embittering it is. . . .

The essential condition for the existence and sway of the bourgeois class, is the formation and augmentation of capital; the condition for capital is wage labour. Wage labour rests exclusively on competition between the labourers. The advance of industry, whose involuntary promoter is the bourgeoisie, replaces the isolation of the labourers, due to competition, by their revolutionary competition, due to association. The development of modern industry, therefore, cuts from under its feet the very foundation on which the bourgeoisie produces and appropriates products. What the bourgeoisie therefore produces, above all, are its own grave-diggers. Its fall and the victory of the proletariat are equally inevitable. . . .

The Communists are distinguished from the other working-class parties by this only: (1) In the national struggles of the proletarians of the different countries, they point out and bring to the front the common interests of the entire proletariat, independent of all nationality. (2) In the various stages of development which the struggle of the working class against the bourgeoisie has to pass through, they always and everywhere represent the interests of the movement as a whole. The Communists, therefore, are on the one hand, practically, the most advanced and resolute section of the working class parties of every country, that section which pushes forward all others; on the other hand, theoretically, they have over the great mass of proletarians the advantage of clearly understanding the line of march, the conditions, and the ultimate general results of the proletarian movement.

The immediate aim of the Communists is the same as that of all the other proletarian parties; formation of the proletariat into a class, overthrow of the bourgeois supremacy, conquest of political power by the proletariat. . . .

We have seen above that the first step in the revolution by the working class is to raise the proletariat to the position of ruling class, to win the battle of democracy.

The proletariat will use its political supremacy to wrest, by degrees, all capital from the bourgeoisie, to centralise all instruments of production in the hands of the state, i.e. of the proletariat organised as the ruling class; and to increase the total of productive forces as rapidly as possible. . . .

When, in the course of development, class distinctions have disappeared, and all production has been concentrated in the hands of a vast association of the whole nation, the public power will lose its political character. Political power, properly so called, is merely the organised power of one class for oppressing another. If the proletariat during its contest with the bourgeoisie is compelled, by the force of circumstances, to organise itself as a class; if, by means of a revolution, it makes itself the ruling class, and, as such, sweeps away by force the old conditions of production, then it will, along with those conditions, have swept away the conditions for the existence of class antagonisms and of classes generally, and will thereby have abolished its own supremacy as a class. In place of the old bourgeois society, with its classes and class antagonisms, we shall have an association, in which the free development of each is the condition for the free development of all.

From Karl Marx and F. Engels, *The Manifesto of the Communist Party* (**8**).

document 2

## EVOLUTIONARY SOCIALISM: BERNSTEIN

The present social order has not been created for all eternity but is subject to the law of change and a catastrophic development with all its horrors and desolation can only be avoided if in legislation consideration is paid to changes in the conditions of production and commerce and to the evolution of the classes. And the number of those who realise this is steadily increasing. Their influence would be much greater than it is today if the social democracy could find the courage to emancipate itself from a phraseology which is actually outworn and if it could make up its mind to appear what it is in reality today: a democratic, socialistic party of reform.

It is not a question of renouncing the so-called right of revolution, this purely speculative right which can be put in no paragraph of a constitution and which no statute book can prohibit, the right which will last as long as the law of nature forces us to die if we abandon the right to breathe. This imprescriptable and inalienable right is as little touched if we place ourselves on the path of reform as the right of self-defence is done away with when we make laws to regulate our personal and property disputes.

But is social democracy today anything beyond a party that strives after the socialist transformation of society by the means of democratic and economic reform?

From *Evolutionary Socialism* (**15**).

## THE REVOLUTIONARY MYTH: SOREL

Syndicalism endeavours to employ methods of expression which throw a full light on things, which put them exactly in the place assigned to them by their nature, and which bring out the whole value of the forces in play. Oppositions, instead of being glozed over, must be thrown into sharp relief if we desire to obtain a clear idea of the Syndicalist movement; the groups which are struggling one against the other must be shown as separate and compact as possible; in short, the movements of the revolted masses must be represented in such a way that the soul of the revolutionaries may receive a deep and lasting impression.

These results could not be produced in any very certain manner by the use of ordinary language; use must be made of a body of images which, by *intuition* alone, and before any considered analyses are made, is capable of evoking as an undivided whole the mass of sentiments which corresponds to the different manifestations of the war undertaken by Socialism against modern society. The Syndicalists solve this problem perfectly, by concentrating the whole of Socialism in the drama of the general strike. . . .

The possibility of the actual realisation of the general strike has been much discussed; it has been stated that the Socialist war could not be decided in one single battle. . . . [I do not] attach any importance to the objections made to the general strike based on considerations of a practical order. The attempt to construct hypotheses about the nature of the struggles of the future and the means of suppressing capitalism, on the model furnished by history, is a return to the old methods of the Utopists. There is no process by which the future can be predicted scientifically. . . . And yet without leaving the present, without reasoning about this future, which seems forever condemned to escape our reason, we should be unable to act at all. Experience shows that the framing of the future, in some indeterminate time may, when it is done in a certain way, be very effective; this happens when the anticipations of the future take the form of those myths which enclose within them all the strongest inclinations of a people, of a party or of a class, inclinations which recur to the mind with the insistence of instincts in all the circumstances of life; and which give an aspect of complete reality to the hopes of immediate action by which, more easily than by any other method, men can reform their desires, passions and mental activity.

The truth of this may be shown by numerous examples. The first Christians expected the return of Christ and the total ruin of the pagan world, with the inauguration of the kingdom of the Saints, at the end of the first generation. This catastrophe did not come to pass, but Christian thought profited so greatly from the apocalyptic myth that certain scholars maintain that the whole preaching of Christ referred solely to this one point.

The myth must be judged as a means of acting in the present; any attempt to discuss how far it can be taken literally as future history is devoid of sense. *It is the myth in its entirety which is alone important*: its parts are only of interest in so far as they bring out the main idea.

... We know that the general strike is indeed what I have said, the myth in which Socialism is wholly comprised, i.e. a body of images capable of evoking instinctively all the sentiments which correspond to the different manifestations of the war undertaken by Socialism against modern society. Strikes have engendered in the proletariat the noblest, deepest and most moving sentiments that they possess: the general strike groups them all in a coordinated picture, and, by bringing them together, gives to each one of them its maximum of intensity; appealing to their painful memories of particular conflicts, it colours with an intense life all the details of the composition presented to consciousness. We thus obtain that intuition of Socialism which language cannot give us with perfect clearness —and we obtain it as a whole, perceived instantaneously.

... Proletarian violence has an entirely different significance from that attributed to it by superficial scholars and by politicians. In the total ruin of institutions and morals there remains something which is powerful, new and intact, and it is that which constitutes, properly speaking, the soul of the revolutionary proletariat.

From G. Sorel, *Reflections on Violence* (**14**).

## REVOLUTIONARY ORGANISATION: LENIN

### a. A party of a new type

We must take upon ourselves the task of organising a universal political struggle under the leadership of *our Party* in such a manner as to obtain all the support possible of all opposition strata for the struggle and for our Party. We must train our Social Democratic practical workers to become political leaders, able to guide all the manifestations of this universal struggle and at the right time to dictate a positive programme of action for the discontented students, for the discontented Zemstvo Councillors, for the discontented religious sects, for the offended elementary school teachers, etc., etc. . . . *the Party* will carry on this universal political agitation, uniting into one inseparable whole the pressure upon the government in the name of the whole people, the revolutionary training of the proletariat—while preserving its political independence—the guidance of the economic struggle of the working class, the utilisation of all its spontaneous conflicts with its exploiters, which rouse and bring into our camp increasing numbers of the proletariat. . . .

Both these tendencies, the opportunist and the 'revolutionary', bow to the prevailing primitiveness; neither believes that it can be eliminated, neither understands our primary and most imperative practical task, namely, to establish *an organisation of revolutionaries* capable of maintaining the energy, the stability and continuity of the political struggle. . . . If we begin with the solid foundation of a strong organisation of revolutionaries, we can guarantee the stability of the movement as a whole and carry out the aims of both Social Democracy and of trade unionism. If, however, we begin with a wide workers' organisation, supposed to be most 'accessible' to the masses, when as a matter of fact it will be most accessible to the gendarmes and will make the revolutionaries most accessible to the police, we shall achieve the aims neither of Social Democracy nor of trade unionism; we shall not escape from our primitiveness. . . .

I assert: (1) that no movement can be durable without a stable organisation of leaders to maintain continuity; (2) that the more widely the masses are spontaneously drawn into the struggle and form the basis of the movement and participate in it, the more necessary is it to have such an organisation and the more stable must it be (for it is much easier for demagogues to sidetrack the more backward sections of the masses); (3) that the organisation must consist chiefly of persons engaged in revolutionary activities as a profession; (4) that in a country with an autocratic government, the more we *restrict* the membership of this organisation to persons who are engaged in revolutionary activities as a profession and who have been professionally trained in the art of combating the political police, the more difficult will it be to catch the organisation, and (5) the *wider* will be the circle of men and women of the working class or of other classes of society able to join the movement and perform active work in it. . . .

Against us it will be argued: such a powerful and strictly secret organisation, which concentrates in its hands all the threads of secret activities, an organisation which of necessity must be a centralised organisation, may too easily throw itself into a premature attack, may thoughtlessly intensify the movement before political discontent, the ferment and anger of the working class, etc., are sufficiently ripe for it. To this we reply: speaking abstractly, it cannot be denied, of course, that a militant organisation *may* thoughtlessly commence a battle, which *may* end in a defeat, which might have been avoided under other circumstances. But we cannot confine ourselves to abstract reasoning on such a question, because every battle bears within itself the abstract possibility of defeat, and there is no other way of *reducing this possibility* than by organised preparation for battle. If, however, we base our argument on the concrete conditions prevailing in Russia at the present time, we must come to the positive conclusion that a strong revolutionary organisation is absolutely necessary precisely for the purpose of giving firmness to the movement, and of *safeguarding* it against the possibility of its making premature attacks. It is precisely at the present time, when no such organisation exists yet, and when the revolutionary movement is rapidly and spontaneously growing, that we *already observe* two opposite extremes (which, as is to be expected, 'meet'), i.e. absolutely unsound Economism and the preaching of moderation, and equally unsound 'excitative terror', which strives artificially to 'call forth symptoms of its end in a movement which is developing and becoming strong, but which is as yet nearer to its beginning than to its end' (V. Zasulich). . . . Only a centralised, militant organisation that consistently carries out a Social Democratic policy, that satisfies, so to speak, all revolutionary instincts and strivings, can safeguard the movement against making thoughtless attacks and prepare it for attacks that hold out the promise of success.

It will be further argued against us that the views on organisation here expounded contradict the 'principles of democracy'. Now, while the first-mentioned accusation was of purely Russian origin, this one is of *purely foreign* origin. . . . Try to put this picture in the frame of our autocracy! Is it possible in Russia for all those 'who accept the principles of the Party programme and render all support they can to the Party' (Rules of the German Social Democratic Party) to control every action of the revolutionary working in secret? Is it possible for all the revolutionaries to elect one of their number to any particular office, when, in the very interests of the work, he *must* conceal his identity from nine out of ten of these 'all'? Ponder a little over the meaning of the high sounding phrases . . . and you will realise that 'broad democracy' in Party organisation, amidst the gloomy autocracy and the domination of gendarme selection, is nothing more than a *useless and harmful toy*. It is a useless toy because, as a matter of fact, no revolutionary organisation has ever practised *broad* democracy, nor could it, however much it desired to do so. It is a harmful toy because any attempt to practise the 'broad democratic principles' will simply facilitate the work of the police in making big raids, it will perpetuate the prevailing primitiveness, divert the thoughts of the practical workers from the serious and imperative task of training themselves to become professional revolutionaries to that of drawing up 'paper' rules for election systems. Only abroad, where very often people who have no opportunity of doing real live work gather together, can the 'game of democracy' be played here and there, especially in small groups.

From V. I. Lenin, *What is to be done?* (**9**).

## b. The dictatorship of the proletariat

The doctrine of the class struggle, as applied by Marx to the question of the state and of the Socialist revolution, leads inevitably to the recognition of the *political rule* of the proletariat, of its dictatorship, i.e. of a power shared with none and relying directly upon the armed force of the masses. The overthrow of the bourgeoisie is realisable only by the transformation of the proletariat into the *ruling class*, able to crush the inevitable and desperate resistance of the bourgeoisie, and to organise, for the new economic order, *all* the toiling and exploited masses. The proletariat needs state power, the centralised organisation of force, the organisation of violence, both for the purpose of crushing the resistance of the exploiters and for the purpose of *guiding* the great mass of the population—the peasantry, the petty bourgeoisie, the semi-proletarians—in the work of organising Socialist economy.

By educating a workers' party, Marxism educates the vanguard of the proletariat, capable of assuming power and of *leading the whole people* to Socialism, of directing and organising the new order, of being the teacher, guide and leader of all the toiling and exploited in the task of building up their social life without the bourgeoisie and against the bourgeoisie. . . .

'The state, i.e. the proletariat organised as the ruling class' —this theory of Marx's is indissolubly connected with all his teaching concerning the revolutionary role of the proletariat in history. The culmination of this role is proletarian dictatorship, the political rule of the proletariat. . . . He who recognises *only* the class struggle is not yet a Marxist. . . . To limit Marxism to the teaching of the class struggle means to curtail Marxism— to distort it, to reduce it to something which is acceptable to the bourgeoisie. A Marxist is one who *extends* the acceptance of class struggle to the acceptance of the *dictatorship of the proletariat.*

Further, the substance of the teachings of Marx about the state is assimilated only by one who understands that the dictatorship of a *single* class is necessary not only for class society generally, not only for the *proletariat* which has overthrown the bourgeoisie, but for the entire *historic period* which separates capitalism from 'classless society', from Communism. The forms of bourgeois states are exceedingly variegated, but their essence is the same: in one way or another, all these states are in the last analysis inevitably a *dictatorship of the bourgeoisie*. The transition from capitalism to Communism will certainly bring about a great variety and abundance of political forms, but the essence will inevitably be only one: the *dictatorship of the proletariat.*

The state will be able to wither away completely when society has realised the rule: 'From each according to his ability; to each according to his needs,' i.e. when people have become accustomed to observe the fundamental rules of social life, and their labour is so productive, that they voluntarily work *according to their ability.* 'The narrow horizon of bourgeois rights,' which compels one to calculate, with the hardheartedness of a Shylock, whether he has not worked half an hour more than another, whether he is not getting less pay than another—this horizon will then be left behind. There will then be no need for any exact calculation by society of the quantity of products to be distributed to each of its members; each will take freely 'according to his needs'.

From the bourgeois point of view, it is easy to declare such a social order 'a pure Utopia'. . . . Even now, most bourgeois 'savants' deliver themselves of such sneers, thereby displaying at once their ignorance and their self-seeking defence of capitalism.

Ignorance—for it has never entered the head of any Socialist to 'promise' that the highest phase of Communism will arrive; while the great Socialists, in *foreseeing* its arrival, presupposed a productivity of labour unlike the present and a person not like the present man in the street, capable of spoiling, without reflection, . . . the stores of social wealth, and of demanding the impossible.

Until the 'higher' phase of Communism arrives, the Socialists demand the *strictest* control, *by society and the state*, of the quantity of labour and the quantity of consumption; only this control must *start* with the expropriation of the capitalists, and must be carried out, not by a state of bureaucrats, but by a state of *armed workers.*

From V. I. Lenin, *State and Revolution* (**10**).

## INTEGRAL NATIONALISM: MAURRAS

La France est déchirée parce que ce qui la gouvernent ne sont pas des hommes d'Etat, mais des hommes de parti. Honnêtes, ils songent seulement au bien d'un parti; malhonnêtes, à remplir leurs poches. Les uns et les autres sont des ennemis de la France. La France n'est pas un parti.

. . .

Il n'y a pas un seul mal, le prolétariat. Il y a deux maux: le prolétariat et le capitalisme. De leur confrontation ressort l'idée de leur antidote commun.

Quel antidote? L'incorporation du prolétariat à la société par l'opération des forces politiques et morales autres que le Capital: les forces du Gouvernement héréditaire, de la corporation et de la Religion, qui ôteront au Capital son brive despotique, l'empêchant de régner tout seul.

. . .

L'idée de nation n'est pas une 'nuée' comme le disent les hurluberlus anarchistes, elle est la représentation en termes abstraits d'une forte realité. La nation est le plus vaste des cercles communautaires qui soient, au temporel, solides et complets. Brisez-le, et vous dénudez l'individu. Il perdra toute sa défense, tous ses appuis, tous ses concours.

Libre de sa nation, il ne le sera ni de la pénurie, ni de l'exploitation, ni de la mort violente. Nous concluons, conformément a la vérité naturelle, que tout ce qu'il est, tout ce qu'il a, tout ce qu'il aime est conditionné par l'existence de la nation: pour peu qu'il veuille se garder, il faut donc qu'il défende coûte que coûte sa nation. Nous ne faisons pas de la nation un Dieu, un absolu metaphysique, mais tout au plus, en quelque sorte, ce que les anciens eussent nommé une deésse. Les Allemandes déifiant l'Allemagne parle de son vieux Dieu, comme de Jéhovah, seul, infini et tout-puissant. Une deésse France entre-naturellement en rapport et composition avec les principes de vie internationale qui peuvent le limiter et l'équilibrier. En un mot, la nation occupe le sommet de la hiérarchie des idées politiques. De ces fortes réalités, c'est la plus forte, voilà tout.

Le nationalisme francais tend à susciter parmi nous une égale religion de la deésse France.

La monarchie héréditaire est en France la constitution naturelle, rationelle, la seule constitution possible du pouvoir central. Sans roi, tout ce que veulent conserver les nationalistes s'affaiblira d'abord et périra ensuite necessairement. Sans roi, tout ce qu'ils veulent reformer durera et s'aggravera ou, à peine détruit, reparaitre sous des formes équivalentes. Condition de toute reforme, la monarchie en est aussi le complément normal et indispensable.

Essentiellement, le royalisme correspond à tous les divers postulats du nationalisme: c'est pour cela qu'il s'est nommé lui même le NATIONALISME INTEGRAL.

From Charles Maurras, *Mes Idées Politiques*, 33e édition: texte établi par Pierre Chardon, Librairie Arthème Fayard, Paris 1937.

**document 6**

**FASCISM: MUSSOLINI**

When in the now distant March of 1919 I summoned to Milan, through the columns of the *Popolo d'Italia*, my surviving supporters who had followed me since the constitution of the Fasces of Revolutionary Action, founded in January 1915, there was no specific doctrinal plan in my mind. I had known and lived through only one doctrine, that of the Socialism of 1903–4 up to the winter of 1914, almost ten years. My experience in this had been that of a follower and of a leader, but not that of a theoretician. My doctrine, even in that period, had been a doctrine of action. An unequivocal Socialism, universally accepted, did not exist after 1905, when the Revisionist Movement began in Germany under Bernstein and there was formed in opposition to that, in the see-saw of tendencies, an extreme revolutionary movement, which in Italy never emerged from the condition of mere words, whilst in Russian Socialism it was the prelude to Bolshevism. Reform, Revolution, Centralization —even the echoes of the terminology are now spent; whilst in the great river of Fascism are to be found the streams which had their source in Sorel, Peguy, in the Lagardelle of the *Mouve-*

*ment Socialiste* and the groups of Italian Syndicalists, who between 1900 and 1914 brought a note of novelty into Italian Socialism. . . .

The years preceding the March on Rome were years during which the necessity of action did not tolerate enquiries or complete elaborations of doctrine. Battles were being fought in the cities and villages. There were discussions, but—and this is more sacred and important—there were deaths. . . . It was precisely in these years that Fascist thought armed itself, refined itself, moving towards one organization of its own. The problems of the individual and the State; the problems of authority and liberty; political and social problems and those more specifically national; the struggle against liberal, democratic, socialist, Masonic, demagogic doctrines was carried on at the same time as the 'punitive expeditions'. But since the 'system' was lacking, adversaries ingenuously denied that Fascism had any power to make a doctrine of its own, while the doctrine rose up, even though tumultuously, at first under the aspect of a violent and dogmatic negation, as happens to all ideas that break new ground, then under the positive aspect of a constructive policy which, during the years of 1926, 1927, 1928, was realised in the laws and institutions of the regime.

Fascism is today clearly defined not only as a regime but as a doctrine. . . . Above all, Fascism, in so far as it considers and observes the political considerations of the moment, believes neither in the possibility nor in the utility of perpetual peace. It thus repudiates the doctrine of Pacifism—born of a renunciation of the struggle and an act of cowardice in the face of sacrifice. War alone brings up to their highest tension all human energies and puts the stamp of nobility upon the peoples who have the courage to meet it. All other trials are substitutes, which never really put a man in front of himself in the alternative of live or death. . . .

Fascism rejects universal concord, and, since it lives in the community of civilised peoples, it keeps them vigilantly and suspiciously before its eyes, it follows their states of mind and the changes in their interests and it does not let itself be deceived by temporary and fallacious appearances.

Such a conception of life makes Fascism the precise negation of that doctrine which formed the basis of so-called Scientific or Marxian Socialism: the doctrine of historical Materialism, according to which the history of human civilisations can be explained only as the struggle of interest between the different social groups and as arising out of changes in the means and instruments of production. That economic improvements—discoveries of raw materials, new methods of work, scientific inventions—should have an importance of their own, no one denies, but that they should suffice to explain human history to the exclusion of all other factors is absurd: Fascism believes, now and always, in holiness and in heroism, that is in acts in which no economic motive—remote or immediate—plays a part. With this negation of historical materialism, according to which men would be only by-products of history, who appear and disappear on the surface of the waves while in the depths the real directive forces are at work, there is also denied the immutable and irreparable 'class struggle' which is the natural product of this economic conception of history, and above all it is denied that the class struggle can be the primary agent of social changes. . . .

After Socialism, Fascism attacks the whole complex of democratic ideologies and rejects them both in their theoretical premises and in their applications or practical manifestations. Fascism denies that the majority, through the mere fact of being a majority, can rule human societies; it denies that this majority can govern by means of a periodical consultation; it affirms the irremediable, fruitful and beneficent inequality of men, who cannot be levelled by such a mechanical and extrinsic fact as universal suffrage. By democratic régimes we mean those in which from time to time the people is given the illusion of being sovereign, while true effective sovereignty lies in other, perhaps irresponsible and secret, forces. Democracy is a régime without a king, but with very many kings, perhaps more exclusive, tyrannical and violent than one king even though a tyrant. This explains why Fascism, although before 1922 for reasons of expediency it made a gesture of republicanism, renounced it before the March on Rome. . . .

Monarchical absolutism is a thing of the past and so is every theocracy. So also feudal privileges and division into impenetrable and isolated castes have had their day. The theory of

Fascist authority has nothing to do with the police state. A party that governs a nation in a totalitarian way is a new fact in history. References and comparisons are not possible. Fascism takes over from the ruins of Liberal Socialistic democratic doctrines those elements which still have a living value. It preserves those that can be called the established facts of history, it rejects all the rest, that is to say the idea of a doctrine which holds good for all times and all peoples. If it is admitted that the nineteenth century has been the century of Socialism, Liberalism and Democracy, it does not follow that the twentieth must also be the century of Liberalism, Socialism and Democracy. Political doctrines pass; peoples remain. It is to be expected that this century may be that of authority, a century of the 'Right', a Fascist century. If the nineteenth century was the century of the individual (Liberalism means individualism) it may be expected that this one may be the century of 'collectivism' and therefore the century of the State. . . .

The keystone of Fascist doctrine is the conception of the State, of its essence, of its tasks, of its ends. For Fascism the State is an absolute before which individuals and groups are relative. Individuals and groups are 'thinkable' in so far as they are within the State. . . .

Fascism desires the State to be strong, organic and at the same time founded on a wide popular basis. The Fascist State has also claimed for itself the field of economics and, through the corporative, social and educational institutions which it has created, the meaning of the State reaches out to and includes the farthest off-shoots; and within the State, framed in their respective organisations, there revolve all the political, economic and spiritual forces of the nation. A State founded on millions of individuals who recognise it, feel it, are ready to serve it, is not the tyrannical state of the mediaeval lord. It has nothing in common with the absolutist states that existed either before or after 1789. In the Fascist State the individual is not suppressed, but rather multiplied, just as in a regiment a soldier is not weakened but multiplied by the number of his comrades. The Fascist State organises the nation, but it leaves sufficient scope to individuals; it has limited useless or harmful liberties and has preserved those that are essential. It cannot be the individual who decides in this matter, but only the State. . . .

For Fascism the tendency to Empire, that is, to the expansion of nations, is a manifestation of vitality; its opposite, staying at home, is a sign of decadence: peoples who rise or re-rise are imperialist, peoples who die are renunciatory. Fascism is the doctrine that is most fitted to represent the aims, the states of mind, of a people, like the Italian people, rising again after many centuries of abandonment or slavery to foreigners. But empire calls for discipline, co-ordination of forces, duty and sacrifice; this explains many aspects of the practical working of the regime and the direction of many of the forces of the State and the necessary severity shown to those who would wish to oppose this spontaneous and destined impulse of the Italy of the twentieth century, to oppose it in the name of the superseded ideologies of the nineteenth, repudiated wherever great experiments of political and social transformation have been courageously attempted: especially where, as now, peoples thirst for authority, for leadership, for order. If every age has its own doctrine, it is apparent from a thousand signs that the doctrine of the present age is Fascism. . . .

From Benito Mussolini, *La Dottrina del Fascismo* (1932) trans. Michael Oakeshott (**21**, pp. 168–78).

**document 7**

**POLITICAL PROPAGANDA: HITLER**

Propaganda must always address itself to the broad masses of the people. For the intellectual classes, or what are called the intellectual classes today, propaganda is not suited, but only scientific exposition. . . . The receptive powers of the masses are very restricted, and their understanding is feeble. On the other hand, they quickly forget. Such being the case, all effective propaganda must be confined to a few bare essentials and these must be expressed as far as possible in stereotyped formulas. These slogans should be persistently repeated until the very last individual has come to grasp the idea that has been put forward. If this principle is forgotten and if an attempt be made to be abstract and general, the propaganda will turn out ineffective; for the public will not be able to digest or retain what is offered to them in this way. Therefore, the greater the scope of the message that has to be presented, the more necessary it is for the propaganda to discover that plan of action which is psychologically the most efficient. . . .

It is not the purpose of propaganda to create a series of alterations in sentiment with a view to pleasing these blasé gentry (i.e. intellectuals). Its chief function is to convince the masses, whose slowness of understanding needs to be given time in order that they may absorb information; and only constant repetition will finally succeed in imprinting an idea on the memory of the crowd. . . .

It is not the business of him who lays down a theoretical programme to explain the various ways in which something can be put into practice. His task is to deal with the problem as such; and, therefore, he has to look to the end rather than the means. The important question is whether an idea is fundamentally right or not. The question of whether or not it may be difficult to carry out in practice is quite another matter. When a man whose task it is to lay down the principles of a programme or policy begins to busy himself with the question as to whether it is expedient and practical, instead of confining himself to a statement of the absolute truth, his work will cease to be a guiding star to those who are looking about for light and leading and will become merely a recipe for everyday life.

From Adolf Hitler, *Mein Kampf* (**18**).

#### THE ARYAN MYTH: HITLER'S VERSION

All the great civilisations of the past became decadent because the originally creative race died out, as a result of contamination of the blood.

The most profound cause of such a decline is to be found in the fact that the people ignored the principle that all culture depends on men, and not the reverse. In other words, in order to preserve a certain culture, the type of manhood that creates such a culture must be preserved. But such a preservation goes hand-in-hand with the inexorable law that it is the strongest and best who must triumph and that they have the right to endure.

He who would live must fight. He who does not wish to fight in this world, where permanent struggle is the law of life, has not the right to exist.

Such a saying may sound hard; but, after all, that is how the matter really stands. Yet far harder is the lot of him who believes that he can overcome nature and in reality insults her. Distress, misery and disease are her rejoinders.

Whoever ignores or despises the laws of race really deprives himself of the happiness to which he believes he can attain. For he places an obstacle in the victorious path of the superior race, and, by so doing, he interferes with a prerequisite condition of all human progress. Loaded with the burden of humanitarian sentiment, he falls back to the level of those who are unable to raise themselves in the scale of being.

It would be futile to discuss the question as to what race or races were the original standard-bearers of human culture and were thereby the real founders of all that we understand by the word, humanity. It is much simpler to deal with this question in so far as it relates to the present time. Here the answer is simple and clear. Every manifestation of human culture, every product of art, science and technical skill, which we see before our eyes today, is almost exclusively the product of the Aryan creative power. This very fact fully justifies the conclusion that it was the Aryan alone who founded a superior type of humanity; therefore he represents the archetype of what we understand by the term: MAN. He is the Prometheus of mankind, from whose shining brow the divine spark of genius has at all times flashed forth, always kindling anew that fire which, in the form of knowledge, illuminated the dark night by drawing aside the veil of mystery and thus showing man how to rise and become master ⸱ all the other beings on the earth. Should he be forced to disappear, a profound darkness will descend on the earth; within a few thousands years human culture will vanish and the world will become a desert. . . .

. . . The Jew offers the most striking contrast to the Aryan. There is probably no other people in the world who have so developed the instinct of self-preservation as the so-called 'chosen' people. The best proof of this statement is found in the simple fact that this race still exists. Where can another people be found that in the course of the last few 1000 years has undergone so few changes in mental outlook and character as the Jewish people? And yet what other people has taken such a constant part in the great revolutions? But even having passed through the most gigantic catastrophes that have overwhelmed mankind, the Jews remain the same as ever. What an infinitely tenacious will to live, to preserve one's kind, is demonstrated by that fact!

The intellectual facilities of the Jew have been trained through 100s (*sic*) of years. Today the Jew is looked upon as specially cunning; and in a certain sense he has been so throughout the ages. His intellectual powers, however, are not the result of an inner evolution but rather have been shaped by the object lessons which the Jew has received from others. . . .

Since the Jew never had a civilisation of his own, he has always been furnished by others with a basis for his intellectual work. His intellect has always developed by the use of those cultural achievements which he has found ready-to-hand around him.

The process has never been the reverse.

For, though among the Jews the instinct of self-preservation has not been weaker but has been much stronger than among other peoples, and though the impression may easily be created that the intellectual powers of the Jew are at least equal to those of other races, the Jews completely lack the most essential prerequisite of a cultural people, namely the idealistic spirit. . . .

That is why the Jewish people, despite the intellectual powers with which they are apparently endowed, have not a culture, certainly not a culture of their own. The culture which the Jew enjoys is the product of the work of others and this product is debased in the hands of the Jew. . . .

. . . The life which the Jew lives as a parasite thriving on the substance of other nations and States has resulted in developing that specific character which Schopenhauer once described, when he spoke of the Jew as 'the Great Master of Lies'. The kind of existence which he lives forces the Jew to the systematic use of falsehood, just as naturally as the inhabitants of northern climates are forced to wear warm clothes. . . .

If we review all the causes which contributed to bring about the downfall of the German people we shall find that the most profound and decisive must be attributed to the lack of insight into the racial problem and especially the failure to recognise the Jewish danger. . . .

How much the whole existence of this people is based on a permanent falsehood is proved in a unique way by 'The Protocols of the Elders of Zion' which are so violently repudiated by the Jews. With groans and moans, the *Frankfurter Zeitung* repeats again and again that these are forgeries. This alone is evidence in favour of their authenticity. What many Jews unconsciously wish to do is here clearly set forth . . . they disclose with an almost terrifying precision, the mentality and methods of action characteristic of the Jewish people and these writings expound in all their various directions the final aims towards which the Jews are striving.

From *Mein Kampf* (**18**).

**document 9**

**THE ORIGINAL PROGRAMME OF THE NAZI PARTY**

Therefore, as we can find a satisfactory solution for the problem of Germany's future only by winning over the broad masses of our people for the support of the national idea, this work of education must be considered the highest and most important task to be accomplished by a movement which does not strive merely to satisfy the needs of the moment but considers itself bound to examine in the light of future results everything it decides to do or refrain from doing.

As early as 1919 we were convinced that the nationalisation of the masses would have to constitute the first and paramount aim of the new movement. From the tactical standpoint, this decision laid a certain number of obligations on our shoulders. 1. No social sacrifice should be considered too great in this effort to win over the masses for the national revival.

In the field of national economics, whatever concessions are granted today to the employees are negligible when compared to the benefit to be reaped by the whole nation if such concessions contribute to bring back the masses of the people once more to the bosom of their own nation.

For a movement which would restore the German worker to the German people it is therefore absolutely necessary to understand clearly that economic sacrifices must be considered light in such cases, provided of course that they do not go to the length of endangering the independence and the stability of the national economic system.

2. The education of the masses along national lines can be carried out only indirectly, by improving their social conditions; for only by such a process can the economic conditions be created which enable everybody to share in the cultural life of the nation.

3. The nationalisation of the broad masses can never be achieved by half-measures—but only by a ruthless and devoted insistence on the one aim which must be achieved. . . .

4. The soul of the masses can only be won if those who lead the movement for that purpose are determined not merely to carry through the positive struggle for their own aims but are also determined to destroy the enemy that opposes them.

. . . The masses are but a part of Nature herself. Their feeling is such that they cannot understand mutual hand-shakings between men who are declared enemies. Their wish is to see the stronger side win and the weaker wiped out or subjected unconditionally to the will of the stronger.

The nationalisation of the masses can be successfully achieved only if, in the positive struggle to win the soul of the people, those who spread the international poison among them are exterminated.

5. All the great problems of our time are problems of the moment and are only the result of certain definite causes. And among all these there is only one that has a profound causal significance. This is the problem of preserving the pure racial stock among the people. . . .

6. By incorporating in the national community the masses of our people who are now in the international camp we do not mean thereby to renounce the principle that the interests of the various trades and professions must be safeguarded. Divergent interests in the various branches of labour and in the trades and professions is not the same as a division between the various

classes, but rather a feature inherent in the economic situation. Vocational grouping does not clash in the least with the idea of a national community; for this means national unity in regard to all those problems that affect the life of the nation as such. . . .

A movement which sincerely endeavours to bring the German worker back into his folk-community, and rescue him from the folly of internationalism, must wage a vigorous campaign against certain notions that are prevalent among the industrialists. One of these notions is that according to the concept of the folk-community the employee is obliged to surrender all his economic rights to the employer and further, that the workers would come into conflict with the folk-community if they should attempt to defend their own just and vital interests. Those who try to propagate such a notion are deliberate liars. The idea of a folk-community does not impose any obligations on the one side that are not imposed on the other.

7. This one-sided but accordingly clear and definite attitude must be manifested in the propaganda of the movement, and on the other hand, this is absolutely necessary to make the propaganda itself effective.

. . . In its message as well as in its form of expression the propaganda must be kept on a level with the intelligence of the masses, and its value must be measured only by the actual success it achieves.

8. The ends which any political reform movement sets out to attain can never be reached by trying to educate the public to influence those in power but only by getting political power into its own hands. Every idea that is meant to move the world has not only the right but the obligation of securing control of the means which will enable the idea to be carried into effect.

9. The nature and internal organisation of the new movement make it anti-parliamentarian. That is to say, it rejects in general and in its own structure all those principles according to which decisions are to be taken on the vote of the majority and according to which the leader is only the executor of the will and opinion of others. The movement lays down the principle that, in the smallest as well as in the greatest problems, one person must have absolute authority and bear all responsibility.

10. The movement steadfastly refuses to take up any stand in

regard to those problems which are either outside of its sphere of political work or seem to have no fundamental importance for us. It does not aim at bringing about a religious reformation, but rather a political reorganisation of our people. It looks upon the two religious denominations as equally valuable mainstays for the existence of our people, and therefore it makes war on all those parties which would degrade this foundation, on which the religious and moral stability of our people is based, to an instrument of party interests.

... The movement does not consider its mission to be the establishment of a monarchy or the preservation of a Republic but rather to create a German State.

11. The problem of the inner organisation of the movement is not one of principle but of expediency.

The best kind of organisation is not that which places a large intermediary apparatus between the leadership of the movement and the individual followers but rather that which works successfully with the smallest possible intermediate apparatus.

12. The future of the movement is determined by the devotion and even intolerance with which its members fight for their cause. They must feel that their cause alone is just, and they must carry it through to success, as against other similar organisations in the same field.

13. The movement ought to educate its adherents to the principle that struggle must not be considered as a necessary evil but as something to be desired in itself. Therefore they must not be afraid of the hostility which their adversaries manifest towards them but they must take it as a necessary condition on which their own right to existence is based.

14. The movement must use all possible means to cultivate respect for the individual personality. It must never forget that all human values are based on personal values, and that every idea and achievement is the fruit of the creative power of one man. We must never forget that admiration for everything that is great is not only a tribute to one creative personality but that all those who feel such admiration become thereby united under one covenant.

From *Mein Kampf* (**18**).

## a. A critical view: Luxemburg

But socialist democracy is not something which begins only in the promised land after the foundations of socialist economy are created; it does not come as some sort of Christmas present for the worthy people who, in the interim, have loyally supported a handful of socialist dictators. Socialist democracy begins simultaneously with the beginnings of the destruction of class rule and of the construction of socialism. It begins at the very moment of the seizure of power by the socialist party. It is the same thing as the dictatorship of the proletariat.

Yes, dictatorship! But this dictatorship consists in the *manner of applying democracy*, not in its *elimination*, in energetic, resolute attacks upon the well entrenched rights and economic relationships of bourgeois society, without which a socialist transformation cannot be accomplished. But this dictatorship must be the work of the *class* and not of a little leading minority in the name of the class—that is, it must proceed step by step out of the active participation of the masses; it must be under their direct influence, subjected to the control of complete public activity; it must arise out of the growing political training of the mass of the people.

Doubtless the Bolsheviks would have proceeded in this very way were it not that they suffered under the frightful compulsion of the world war, the German occupation and all the abnormal difficulties connected therewith, things which were inevitably bound to distort any socialist policy, however imbued it might be with the best intentions and the finest principles.

A crude proof of this is provided by the use of terror to so wide an extent by the Soviet government, especially in the most recent period just before the collapse of German imperialism, and just after the attempt on the life of the German ambassador. The commonplace to the effect that revolutions are not pink teas is in itself pretty inadequate.

Everything that happens in Russia is comprehensible and represents an inevitable chain of causes and effects, the starting point and end term of which are: the failure of the German proletariat and the occupation of Russia by German imperialism. It would be demanding something superhuman from Lenin and his comrades if we should expect of them that under such circumstances they should conjure forth the finest democracy, the most exemplary dictatorship of the proletariat and a flourishing socialist economy. By their determined revolutionary stand, their exemplary strength in action, and their unbreakable loyalty to international socialism, they have contributed whatever could possibly be contributed under such devilishly hard conditions. The danger begins only when they make a virtue of necessity and want to freeze into a complete theoretical system all the tactics forced upon them by these fatal circumstances and want to recommend them to the international proletariat as a model of socialist tactics. When they get in their own light in this way, and hide their genuine, unquestionable historical service under the bushel of false steps forced upon them by necessity, they render a poor service to international socialism for the sake of which they have fought and suffered; for they want to place in its new storehouse as new discoveries all the distortions prescribed in Russia by necessity and compulsion—in the last analysis only by-products of the bankruptcy of international socialism in the present world war.

Let the German Government Socialists cry that the rule of the Bolsheviks in Russia is a distorted expression of the dictatorship of the proletariat.

From Rosa Luxemburg, *The Russian Revolution* (**16**).


### b. Conditions of admission into the Communist International: Stalin

It is impossible to win and maintain the dictatorship of the proletariat without a Party made strong by its cohesion and discipline. But iron discipline cannot be thought of without unity of will and absolutely united action on the part of all members of the Party. This does not mean that the possibility of a conflict of opinion within the Party is excluded. Discipline, indeed, far from excluding criticism and conflict of opinion, presupposes their existence. But this most certainly does not imply that there should be 'blind discipline'. Discipline does

101

not exclude but presupposes *understanding*, voluntary submission, for only a conscious discipline can be a discipline of iron. But when discussion has been closed and a decision made, unity in will and action is the indispensable condition without which there can be neither Party nor discipline.

In the present epoch of intensification of civil war, the Communist Party can only accomplish its task if it is organised on a basis of centralism, ruled by an iron, almost military discipline, directed by a central organism possessing strong authority, commanding extensive powers and enjoying the general confidence of the members of the Party.

### c. The Party and factions: Stalin

'To weaken, however little, the iron discipline in the Party of the proletariat (particularly during its dictatorship) means giving effective aid to the bourgeoisie against the proletariat.'

(Lenin: *'Left-Wing' Communism*)

It follows that the existence of factions is incompatible with the unity and discipline of the Party. It is obvious that it leads to the existence of several centres of direction, and so to the absence of a general directing body, to division in the united will that should direct the carrying out of the Party's tasks, to the under-mining of discipline, and to the weakening of the dictatorship. It is true that the parties of the Second International which oppose the dictatorship and have no intention of leading the proletarians to the conquest of power, can permit themselves the luxury of factions, for they have no need of an iron discipline. But the parties of the Communist International, which organise their activity with a view to the conquest of power and the maintenance of the dictatorship of the proletariat, cannot afford this luxury. The Party as a united Will must exclude every tendency to form factions, to divide power within it.

The opportunist elements of the Party are the source of factions. . . . All these groups penetrate somehow or other into the Party, into which they introduce the spirit of opportunism. They represent the chief source of faction-forming and division. They disorganise the party, undermining it from within. To begin the battle with Imperialism with such 'allies' as these is to open oneself to simultaneous attack from front and rear. It is necessary, therefore, to conduct a ruthless fight against these opportunist elements, and not to hesitate to expel them from the Party. . . .

It (i.e. the Communist Party) has succeeded in creating internal unity and in welding its ranks powerfully together above all because it was able to purify itself in time from pollution with opportunism, and to expel the liquidators and the Mensheviks. The proletarian parties, in order to develop and grow strong, must get rid of the opportunists and reformists, the social-Imperialists and Socialist-jingoes, the social-patriots and the social-pacifists. The Party will make itself strong by freeing itself from opportunist elements.

From *The Theory and Practice of Leninism* trans. and publ. by the C.P.G.B., 1925.


**documents 11a, b**

**THE COMMUNIST VIEW OF FASCISM**

**a. Stalin**

It is not true that Fascism is only a militant organisation of the *bourgeoisie*. . . . Fascism is the militant organisation of the *bourgeoisie* which bases itself on the active support of Social Democracy. Objectively, Social Democracy is the moderate wing of Fascism. There is no reason to suppose that the militant organisation of the *bourgeoisie* can achieve any decisive successes . . . without active support from Social Democracy. There is just as little ground to think that Social Democracy could achieve decisive successes . . . without the active support of that militant organisation of the *bourgeoisie*. Those organisations do not contradict but supplement one another. They are not antipodes but twins. . . . Fascism is the shapeless political *bloc* of these two basic organisations, a *bloc* that has emerged in the post-war crisis of imperialism for the struggle against proletarian revolution.

## b. Trotsky

It is [our] duty to sound the alarm: the leadership of the Comintern is leading the German proletariat towards an enormous catastrophe, the core of which is the panicky capitulation before Fascism. The coming into power of the German National Socialists would mean above all the extermination of the flower of the German proletariat, the disruption of its organisations, the extirpation of its belief in itself and in its future. Considering the far greater . . . acuteness of the social antagonisms in Germany, the hellish work of Italian Fascism would probably appear as a pale and almost humane experiment in comparison with the work of German national socialism. . . .

Workers, Communists, . . . should Fascism come to power it will ride over your skulls and spines like a terriffic tank. Your salvation lies in merciless struggle. And only a fighting unity with Social Democratic workers can bring victory. Make haste, you have very little time left!

Quoted by I. Deutscher in *Stalin* (**32**, pp. 406–9).

**document 12**
### NAZISM IN POWER: THE ASSESSMENT OF THE BRITISH AMBASSADOR

The Nazi Party and the Press were still hard at work at that time (1937) beating the anti-Bolshevist drum, mainly for purposes of internal consumption, but also with a view to making the outside world believe that Germany was the sole bulwark against universal Communism. The opportunity offered by Japan's bad relations with Russia had been seized in the preceding year to sign the German-Japanese agreement. This so-called anti-Communist, but equally anti-democratic, front was to become a triangular one towards the end of 1937, when Italy joined it. The ten-year German-Polish Agreement had been signed in 1934, and thus, by 1937, Germany, so far from being friendless in the world, as she was so apt, in self-commiseration, to depict herself to be, had greatly fortified her political situation. The success of Nazism was attracting many sympathisers abroad, particularly in Hungary, with irredenta of her own, but also in other European countries, as well as overseas. The *Auslandsdeutschen*, or Germans living in foreign countries, were busily organising themselves abroad in support of the movement in the fatherland, and as an advance-guard for political invasion by that fatherland. It was the heyday of the movement and of Hitler himself. Though there might be restiveness in Germany itself at the exactions of the Party and the recurring food shortages, the Germans are a docile, credulous, and disciplined people who like being governed, and they comforted themselves with the assurance that Hitler had the knack of getting everything he wanted without war. Above all, the malleable German youth were enthusiastic over a movement which appealed so strongly to the young, and were being taught to accord to Hitler the attributions of something very nearly akin to God. When people lightly talk of the German nation overthrowing its present rulers, it must be borne in mind that for nearly seven years the whole of the German youth has been taught the cult of force and power, and that they are Hitler's most devoted adherents in its worship.

. . .

Nobody who has not witnessed the various displays given at Nuremberg during the week's rally, or been subjected to the atmosphere thereat, can be said to be fully acquainted with the Nazi movement in Germany. It was an extremely necessary and useful experience, and not a single moment of my time during the two days I was there was left unoccupied. In addition to attending the review of the party leaders, 140,000 in number, and representing at that time over two million members of the Party (a year later, again at Nuremberg, Hitler was to tell me himself that there were well over three million Party officials); a rally of the Hitler youth, 48,000 strong with 5000 girls; and at a supper party in Herr Himmler's S.S. camp of 25,000 blackshirts, I had talks with Hitler himself, Neurath, Goering and Goebbels, as well as a number of other less important personages.

The displays themselves were most impressive. That of the Party leaders (or heads of the Party organisation in towns and villages throughout the country) took place in the evening at eight p.m., in the stadium or Zeppelinfeld. Dressed in their brown shirts, these 140,000 men were drawn up in six great columns, with passages between them, mostly in the stadium itself, but filling also the tiers of seats surrounding the stadium and facing the elevated platform reserved for the Chancellor, his Ministers and his guards, the massed bands, official guests, and other spectators. Hitler himself arrived at the far entrance of the stadium, some 400 yards from the platform, and, accompanied by several hundred of his followers, marched on foot up the central passage to his appointed place. His arrival was theatrically notified by the sudden turning into the air of the 300 or more searchlights with which the stadium was surrounded. The blue-tinged light from these met thousands of feet up in the sky at the top to make a kind of square roof, to which a chance cloud gave added realism. The effect, which was both solemn and beautiful, was like being inside a cathedral of ice. At the word of command the standard-bearers then advanced from out of sight at the far end, up the main lane, and over the further tiers and up the four side lanes. A certain proportion of these standards had electric lights on their shafts, and the spectacle of these five rivers of red and gold rippling forward under the dome of blue light, in complete silence, through the massed formations of brownshirts, was indescribably picturesque. I had spent six years in St Petersburg before the war in the best days of the old Russian ballet, but for grandiose beauty I have never seen a ballet to compare with it. The German, who has a highly developed herd instinct, is perfectly happy when he is wearing a uniform, marching in step, and singing in chorus, and the Nazi revolution has certainly known how to appeal to these instincts in his nature. As a display of aggregate strength it was ominous; as a triumph of mass organisation combined with beauty it was superb.

From Sir Nevile Henderson, *Failure of a Mission*, Hodder & Stoughton, 1940.

**ANARCHISM IN POWER: ORWELL'S IMPRESSIONS OF CATALONIA**

The Anarchists were still in virtual control of Catalonia and the revolution was still in full swing. To anyone who had been there since the beginning it probably seemed even in December or January (1936–7) that the revolutionary period was ending; but when one came straight from England the aspect of Barcelona was something startling and overwhelming. It was the first time that I had ever been in a town where the working class was in the saddle. Practically every building of any size had been seized by the workers and was draped with red flags or with the red and black flag of the Anarchists; every wall was scrawled with the hammer and sickle and with the initials of the revolutionary parties; almost every church had been gutted and its images burnt. Churches here and there were being systematically demolished by gangs of workmen. Every shope and café had an inscription saying that it had been collectivised; even the bootblacks had been collectivised and their boxes painted red and black. Waiters and shop-walkers looked you in the face and treated you as an equal. Servile and even ceremonial forms of speech had temporarily disappeared. Nobody said '*Señor*' or '*Don*' or even '*Usted*'; everyone called everyone else 'Comrade' and 'Thou', and said '*Salud!*' instead of '*Buenos días*'. Tipping was forbidden by law; almost my first experience was receiving a lecture from a hotel manager for trying to tip a lift-boy. There were no private motor-cars, they had all been commandeered, and all the trams and taxis and much of the other transport were painted red and black. The revolutionary posters were everywhere, flaming from the walls in clean reds and blues that made the few remaining advertisements look like daubs of mud. Down the Ramblas, the wide central artery of the town where crowds of people streamed constantly to and fro, the loudspeakers were bellowing revolutionary songs all day and far into the night. And it was the aspect of the crowds that was the queerest thing of all. In outward appearance it was a town in which the wealthy classes had practically ceased to exist. Except for a small number of women and foreigners there were no 'well-dressed' people at all. Practically everyone wore rough working-class clothes, or blue overalls, or some variant of the militia uniform. All this was queer and moving. There was much in it that I did not understand, in some ways I did not even like it, but I recognised it immediately as a state of affairs worth fighting for. Also I believed that things were as they appeared, that this was really a workers' State and that the entire bourgeoisie had either fled, been killed, or voluntarily come over to the workers' side; I did not realise that great numbers of well-to-do bourgeois were simply lying low and disguising themselves as proletarians for the time being.

Together with all this there was something of the evil atmosphere of war. The town had a gaunt untidy look, roads and buildings were in poor repair, the streets at night were dimly lit for fear of air-raids, the shops were mostly shabby and half-empty. Meat was scarce and milk practically unobtainable, there was a shortage of coal, sugar, and petrol, and a really serious shortage of bread. Even at this period the bread-queues were often hundreds of yards long. Yet so far as one could judge the people were contented and hopeful. There was no unemployment, and the price of living was still extremely low; you saw very few conspicuously destitute people, and no beggars except the gipsies. Above all, there was a belief in the revolution and in the future, a feeling of having suddenly emerged into an era of equality and freedom. Human beings were trying to behave as human beings and not as cogs in the capitalist machine. In the barbers' shops were Anarchist notices (the barbers were mostly Anarchists) solemnly explaining that barbers were no longer slaves. In the streets were coloured posters appealing to prostitutes to stop being prostitutes. To anyone from the hard-boiled, sneering civilisation of the English-speaking races there was something rather pathetic in the literalness with which these idealistic Spaniards took the hackneyed phrases of revolution.

. . .

Everyone who has made two visits, at intervals of months, to Barcelona during the war has remarked upon the extraordinary changes that took place in it. And curiously enough, whether they went there first in August and again in January, or, like myself, first in December and again in April, the thing they said was always the same: that the revolutionary atmosphere had vanished. No doubt to anyone who had been there in August, when the blood was scarcely dry in the streets and the militia were quartered in the smart hotels, Barcelona in December would have seemed bourgeois; to me, fresh from England, it was liker to a workers' city than anything I had conceived possible. Now the tide had rolled back. Once again it was an ordinary city, a little pinched and chipped by war, but with no outward signs of working-class predominance.

From George Orwell, *Homage to Catalonia* (**20,** pp. 8–10 and 106).

# Bibliography

GENERAL WORKS

1  Wiskemann, E. *Europe of the Dictators*, Collins 1967.
2  Gilbert, M. *The European Powers* 1900–45, Weidenfeld and Nicolson 1965.
3  Mosse, G. L. *The Culture of Western Europe*, Murray 1963.
4  Cole, G. D. H. *A History of Socialist Thought*: Vol. 4 *Communism and Social Democracy 1914–1931*; Vol. 5 *Socialism and Fascism 1931–1939*, Macmillan 1953–1960.
5  Lipset, S. *Political Man*, Heinemann 1963.
6  Laqueur, W. *Russia and Germany: a century of conflict*, Weidenfeld & Nicolson 1965.
7  *The Journal of Contemporary History*: particularly Vol. 1 no. 1, 'International Fascism 1920–45' and no. 2, 'Left-wing intellectuals between the wars'; Weidenfeld and Nicolson 1966–7.


PRIMARY SOURCES

8  Marx, K. and Engels, F. *The Manifesto of the Communist Party*, English edition, 1888 (available in several editions, e.g. *The Essential Left*, Unwin Books 1960; with an introduction by A. J. P. Taylor, Penguin Books).
9  Lenin, V. I. *What is to be done?*
10  Lenin, V. I. *State and Revolution*.
11  Lenin, V. I. *'Left-Wing' Communism*.
12  Lenin, V. I. *Two Tactics*.
   Lenin's works are available in a number of English editions, both separately and collected, e.g. the Little Lenin Library, Lawrence and Wishart 1933; the Foreign Languages Press, Peking 1965. *State and Revolution* is also printed in *The Essential Left*, see above.
13  Stalin, J. V. *Leninism*, Little Stalin Library, Lawrence & Wishart 1940.

14  Sorel, G. *Reflections on Violence*, trans. T. E. Hulme, Allen & Unwin 1915.

15  Bernstein, E. *Evolutionary Socialism*, trans. Edith C. Harvey, Schocken Books, New York 1961.

16  Luxemburg, R. *The Russian Revolution* (and) *Leninism or Marxism*, trans. Bertram D. Wolfe, University of Michigan Press 1961.

17  Mussolini, B. *My Autobiography*, Scribners 1928.

18  Hitler, A. *Mein Kampf*, trans. J. Murphy, Hurst & Blackett 1939.

19  Hitler, A. *Speeches of Adolf Hitler*, ed. N. H. Baynes, Oxford University Press 1942.

20  Orwell, G. *Homage to Catalonia*, Penguin 1962.

21  Oakeshott, M. *The Social and Political Doctrines of Contemporary Europe*, Cambridge University Press 1950.

THE LEFT

22  Caute, D. *The Left in Europe since 1789*, Weidenfeld & Nicolson 1966.

23  Berlin, I. *Karl Marx*, Oxford University Press 1963.

24  Lichtheim, G. *Marxism*, Routledge & Kegan Paul 1961.

25  Carew Hunt, R. N. *The Theory and Practice of Communism*, Bles 1950.

26  Cole, G. D. H. *Marxism and Anarchism*, Macmillan 1957.

27  Wilson, E. *To the Finland Station*, Secker and Warburg 1961.

28  Wolfe, B. D. *Three Who Made a Revolution* (*Lenin, Trotsky, Stalin*), Thames and Hudson 1956.

29  Hill, C. *Lenin and the Russian Revolution*, English Universities Press 1947.

30  Trotsky, L. *The History of the Russian Revolution*, Gollancz 1932–3.

31  Carr, E. H. *A History of Soviet Russia*, Macmillan 1950–3.

32  Deutscher, I. *Stalin: a political biography*, Oxford University Press 1967; Penguin Books.

33  Daniels, R. V. *The Stalin Revolution: fulfilment or betrayal of Communism?* Heath 1965.

34  Schapiro, L. *The Communist Party of the Soviet Union*, Eyre & Spottiswoode 1960.

35  Toynbee, A., ed. *The Impact of the Russian Revolution 1917–1967*, Oxford University Press 1967.

111

**36** Deutscher, I. *The Unfinished Revolution*, Oxford University Press 1967.

**37** Drachkovitch, M., ed. *The Revolutionary Internationals*, Stanford University Press, California 1966.

**38** Nettl, J. *Rosa Luxemburg*, Oxford University Press 1966.

**39** Curtis, M. *Three Against the Third Republic: Sorel, Barres and Maurras*, Oxford University Press 1960.

**40** Caute, D. *Communism and the French Intellectuals*, Deutsch 1964.

**41** Pelling, H. *The British Communist Party*, A. and C. Black 1958.

**42** Joll, J. *The Anarchists*, Eyre & Spottiswoode 1964.

**43** Crossman, R., ed. *The God that Failed*, Harper 1949.

**44** Lowenthal, R. *World Communism: the disintegration of a secular faith*, Oxford University Press 1964.

**45** Cohn-Bendit, D. and Cohn-Bendit, G. *Obsolete Communism: the left-wing alternative*, Penguin Books 1968.

THE RIGHT

**46** Carsten, F. L. *The Rise of Fascism*, Batsford 1967.

**47** Weber, E. and Rogger, H., ed. *The European Right*, Weidenfeld & Nicolson 1965.

**48** Nolte, E. *Three Faces of Fascism*, Weidenfeld & Nicolson 1965.

**49** Fermi, L. *Mussolini*, Chicago University Press 1961.

**50** Finer, H. *Mussolini's Italy*, Cass 1964.

**51** Hibbert, C. *Benito Mussolini*, Longmans 1962.

**52** Deakin, F. W. *The Brutal Friendship: Mussolini, Hitler and the Fall of Italian Fascism*, Weidenfeld & Nicolson 1962.

**53** Mosse, G. L. *The Crisis of German Ideology: intellectual origins of the Third Reich*, Weidenfeld & Nicolson 1966.

**54** Bullock, A. *Hitler: a study in tyranny*, Odhams 1952, Penguin Books 1962.

**55** Allen, W. S. *The Nazi Seizure of Power*, Eyre & Spottiswoode 1966.

**56** Shirer, W. L. *The Rise and Fall of the Third Reich*, Secker & Warburg 1960.

**57** Snell, J. L., ed. *The Nazi Revolution: Germany's Guilt or Germany's Fate?*, Heath 1959.

**58** Schoenbaum, D. *Hitler's Social Revolution*, Weidenfeld & Nicolson 1967.

**59** Reitlinger, G. *The S.S.: alibi of a nation*, Heinemann 1956.

**60** Trevor-Roper, H. *The Last Days of Hitler*, Macmillan 1947.
**61** Wright, G. *France in Modern Times*, Murray 1962.
**62** Weber, E. *Action française*, Stanford University Press 1962.
**63** Cross, C. *The Fascists in Britain*, Barrie & Rockliff 1961.
**64** Mosley, Sir O. *My Life*, Nelson 1968.
**65** Thomas, H. *The Spanish Civil War*, Eyre & Spottiswoode 1961.
**66** Payne, S. G. *Falange*, Stanford University Press 1961.
**67** Macartney, C. A. *October Fifteenth: a History of Modern Hungary*,
Edinburgh University Press 1957.
**68** Brook-Shepherd, G. *Dollfuss*, Macmillan 1961.

# Index

# Index